Mandela

IN CELEBRATION OF A GREAT LIFE

For Matthew, Leila, Morne and Gabriella Ruby

Mandela

IN CELEBRATION OF A GREAT LIFE

Charlene Smith

Foreword by Archbishop Desmond Tutu

STRUIK TRAVEL & HERITAGE

Published by Struik Travel & Heritage
(an imprint of Random House Struik (Pty) Ltd)
Company Reg. No. 1966/003153/07
Wembley Square, First Floor, Solan Road, Gardens, Cape Town, 8001, South Africa
PO Box 1144, Cape Town, 8000, South Africa
www.randomstruik.co.za

First published in 1999, reprinted 2000 (hard cover)
Second edition published in 2003 (hard cover)
Third edition published in 2005 (hard cover and soft cover)
Fourth edition published in 2012 (soft cover)
Copyright © in published edition: Random House Struik 1999, 2003, 2005, 2012
Copyright © in text: Charlene Smith 1999, 2003, 2005, 2012
Copyright © in photographs: see credits on page 171, 1999, 2003, 2005, 2012

Publisher: Claudia Dos Santos
Managing editor: Roelien Theron
Editor: Leah van Deventer
Co-editor: Charlene Smith
Designer: Catherine Coetzer
Picture researcher: Colette Stott
Project coordinator: Alana Bolligelo
Indexer: Joy Clack
Proofreader: Alfred LeMaitre
Reproduction by Hirt & Carter Cape (Pty) Ltd
Printed and bound Tien Wah Press (Pte.) Limited, Singapore

ISBN 978 1 43170 079 0 (Print)
ISBN 978 1 43170 238 1 (ePub)
ISBN 978 1 43170 239 8 (PDF)

10 9 8 7 6 5 4 3 2 1

More than 50 000 unique African images are available to purchase from our image bank
at www.imagesofafrica.co.za

PUBLISHER'S NOTES

- Where no reliable sources could be found, names have been omitted.
- The opinions expressed in this book are those of the author and do not necessarily
  reflect the opinions of the publisher.
- The terms 'black' and 'African' refer to all people that were not born with white skins.
  However, in this book, to explain certain peculiarities of laws or events, or in quoting
  sources directly, the terms 'coloured' and 'Indian' are on occasion used.
- Every effort has been made to trace the owners of copyrighted material and to seek
  their permission for the use thereof. The publisher apologises for any inadvertent
  omissions and would be grateful if notified of any corrections, which shall be included
  in future reprints and editions of the book.
- Please email any comments or updates to: mandela_greatlife@randomstruik.co.za

HALF-TITLE PAGE: Mandela and his wife Graça Machel wave to crowds at the 46664 AIDS
benefit concert in Cape Town in 2003.

TITLE PAGE: Mandela at the 2007 unveiling ceremony of a bronze statue in his honour at
London's Parliament Square.

RIGHT: Mandela stands with Britain's Prince Richard, the Duke of Gloucester, at his
investiture as a Bailiff Grand Cross of the Order of St John, in London, 2004.

Contents

Foreword

ABOVE: His Holiness the 14th Dalai Lama greets Archbishop Desmond Tutu in Vancouver, 2004.

IN JULY 1988, two years before Nelson Mandela walked a free man from Victor Verster Prison, Archbishop Trevor Huddleston suggested, in his role as the President of the Anti-Apartheid Movement, that the world should celebrate Mandela's 70th birthday in prison. Many thousands of young people especially, although not exclusively, responded enthusiastically to his call to make this the mother of all birthday celebrations. People of all ages went on pilgrimage from all the corners of the United Kingdom and then they gathered at Hyde Park Corner in London, an enormous sea of faces. They congregated there, 250,000 of them, and the vast majority were young people.

What struck me forcibly, as I gazed over them, was that most of them had not even been born when Madiba was sentenced to life imprisonment in 1963, and they had not seen him since; they had not heard from him, but they had certainly heard about him from others. The point is that they had no direct knowledge of him and, since pictures of prisoners were not permitted, they did not know what he really looked like even now. And yet here they were paying tribute to a prisoner, yes a prisoner, of conscience whom the British Prime Minister Margaret Thatcher (of the time) had disdainfully dismissed as a terrorist.

What an extraordinary phenomenon that he was able to move people so deeply without saying anything, without doing anything. Some of us worried that they might be in for an enormous disillusionment, that they would discover that their idol had feet of clay. Perhaps it would be better that he should remain incarcerated, out of sight, because distance did indeed lend enchantment to the view. In prison he was serving a splendid purpose because he was giving focus to the struggle, personalising it in that way so essential for causes if they were to galvanise the kind of popular support that the largely indifferent Reagan White House and Thatcher 10 Downing Street would find difficult to ignore. Outside prison he would be found to be less effective because he would be so human, so vulnerable, so disappointing to those who had placed him on a pedestal of near sainthood and infallibility.

Yes, we were all in the seventh heaven of delight on 11 February 1990, when he walked out of Victor Verster prison side by side with Winnie. It was an unforgettable day, but there were butterflies in the pit of the stomach – would he measure up to all that people believed and hoped about him? Would we not all come crashing to the ground after all the euphoria? The world joined us in welcoming the world's most famous prisoner, but for how long would they pay attention when they are so notoriously fickle? Was he but a few days' wonder, and would they flit off to the next attraction to land in their spotlight?

The man is a phenomenon, in a class by himself, for the frenzy of media attention has not abated. If anything, it has increased. Far from being a huge disillusionment, he has not ceased to amaze everyone. A deeply divided land, alienated by long years of repression and injustice, and at variance on most subjects, is unanimous about one thing: that this former terrorist, so frequently vilified and hated, is today our greatest asset.

He is loved by virtually all South Africans, even the most virulent critics of his African National Congress-led government. He is the most popular political leader in the land, almost beyond criticism. Who will easily forget the scenes at Ellis Park when he walked onto the turf wearing François Pienaar's No. 6 on his Springbok jersey on the day of the final for the Rugby

World Cup in 1995, when an overwhelmingly white crowd, mostly Afrikaners, broke out in reverberating chants: 'Nelson, Nelson, Nelson'. He has the knack of doing the right thing, which with some political leaders would be contrived or gauche. With him it turns out to be exactly what touches responsive chords in the people. He has bowled South Africans, and indeed the world, over with his extraordinary magnanimity, his readiness and eagerness to forgive. He invited the widows of former South African political leaders of all persuasions and races to a tea party at the Presidency and charmed them. He stole the hearts of many Afrikaners, whom he had already attracted by supporting the Springbok emblem for rugby, by going to visit the widow of Dr Verwoerd in her Afrikaner exclusivist stronghold – Orania. Here he was having tea, at some inconvenience to himself, with the widow of the architect and high priest of apartheid. Unbelievable! He later had a meal with Dr Percy Yutar, the man who had prosecuted in the Rivonia Trial and who many believed had gone well beyond the accepted conventions in passionately demanding the death sentence for the accused (of whom he was one). His magnanimity knows no bounds. He was ready to have accompanied Mr PW Botha to appear before the TRC as subpoenaed, if it would help Mr Botha not feel humiliated.

An interesting mix of genuine humility and a regal sense of his position, he is at pains to say he is no saint and just an ordinary member of the ANC, a consensus man. And he can appear in court because he has a high sense of the law and stood for two days to demonstrate that respect. But he can be short with those who are presumptuous with regard to his office, not his person. He undoubtedly is our greatest gift and asset. God blessed us wonderfully in giving him to us at this period in our history – he has helped to hold together a fractious lot. God's sense of humour is huge. Here is the terrorist par excellence whom some of the high and mighty in former days spurned. Now everyone rushes to South Africa on state or other visits, just to have a photo opportunity with the world's most admired statesman. Some people might want the earth to open up so that their leaders might disappear out of sight – we stand tall because we have a transparently good man as our President. A European Prime Minister urged me to try to get Mandela to visit his country to say farewell. I know many other countries would consider it a great honour if he came before his retirement. No one else that I know as head of state has been asked to so many regional summits to take leave of his fellow heads of state in Europe, Africa, Latin America and Asia.

He has left us a wonderful legacy – to strive to become increasingly one people with diverse cultures, languages, beliefs of different races and so on – the rainbow people of South Africa – and we owe him an enormous debt of gratitude. He has laid a good and firm foundation. It is up to all of us to make sure we build a structure that will stand the buffetings of fate. That would be the only fitting monument to him.

Archbishop Desmond Tutu, 1998

ABOVE: Outspoken Archbishop Desmond Tutu, a friend and counsellor to Nelson Mandela, is often considered the conscience of South Africa, while Mandela is seen as its heart.

Author's note

*I come from a culture where
traditionally, children are seen as
both our present and our future,
so I have always believed it is our
responsibility as adults to give
children futures worth having.*

Graça Machel
Report on the Impact
of Armed Conflict on Children,
United Nations, 1996

MY SON WAS A TALL 14-YEAR-OLD when this book was launched in 1999 at a gala event that saw Nelson Mandela, Graça Machel, Josina Machel, Zenani Mandela and members of their families attend. Former constitutional negotiator Cyril Ramaphosa was there and so was future South African president, Jacob Zuma. Matthew was shy as teenagers often are. But at one stage, when the joy of onstage dancers and the beat of music got to Madiba – as it often did – he stepped across to our table which was next to his and held out his hand to Matthew. The two jived in front of the hundreds that attended.

I had no camera to record that event, but others took photographs of us with Madiba and his family. It was such a joyous evening; in it was the promise of our new South Africa. It seemed to confirm what Alexis de Tocqueville wrote in his seminal book, *Democracy in America*, 'The social order overthrown by a revolution is almost always better than the one immediately preceding it, and experience teaches us that, generally speaking, the most perilous moment for a bad government is one when it seeks to mend its ways … a grievance comes to appear intolerable once the possibility of removing it crosses men's minds.'

But promises can remain just that. Liberators can lift the robes cast aside by old oppressors and find they fit just fine. South Africa today is in the perilous stage writers like De Tocqueville warned of, where democracy in all its messy enthusiasm challenges old-style autocracy. New leaders may find that, once in power, their popularity diminishes; criticism is more frequent than praise. And so it should be, for democracy to prevail.

However, whichever way the pendulum of democracy swings for South Africa, none can doubt the impact that the confluence of remarkable individuals had at a certain brief time in the country; people including Nobel Prize winners Archbishop Emeritus Desmond Tutu, Frederik Willem de Klerk, Nadine Gordimer and, of course, Nelson Mandela. It was my privilege to report on South Africa during its darkest days, and those of its greatest light.

No book is possible without the work of librarians and so I salute the staff at two national treasures, the Mayibuye Centre at the University of the Western Cape and the South African National Library in Cape Town; on their shelves I found gems. My children, Leila and Matthew, remain my inspiration, while my granddaughter, Gabriella Ruby, teaches me anew about the joy inherent in every day and the importance of treading lightly upon our fragile earth.

This book is critical of Mandela in some respects. He has made it clear that he does not seek fawning praise, and history will not permit it. What do I admire most about Nelson Mandela? It is this: in societies where class makes some people (such as security guards, cleaners and waiters) 'invisible', and where most fail to acknowledge their presence, Mandela will clasp them by the hand and ask about their lives. If he sees them again he will remember them and the details they shared. He is not a sound-bite politician, he actually cares, and once he has met you he will never forget your name.

Every ordinary person who has met Mandela has been made to feel special by him. His actions embodied the meaning behind the Hindu greeting of Namaste – the god in me honours the god in you. Be kind, it costs little and its rewards are great.

Charlene Smith, Cambridge, Massachusetts, 2012

Mandela's life

1918
JULY 18: Rolihlahla Mandela is born into the Thembu tribe to Gadla Henry Mphakanyiswa and Nosekeni Fanny, in the Eastern Cape village of Mvezo.

1927
After his father's death, Mandela falls under the care of his uncle Chief Jongintaba Dalindyebo, who sends him to missionary schools (where he receives his English name, Nelson). Mandela receives a thorough grounding in Xhosa culture, history and the duties implicit in governance.

1930s
Mandela begins his tertiary education at the University of Fort Hare, and is elected onto the Students' Representative Council. He meets Oliver Tambo and the two join a protest boycott and are suspended from the institute.

1940s
Fleeing an arranged marriage, Mandela goes to Johannesburg, where he completes his BA and goes on to study Law at the University of the Witwatersrand. He joins the African National Congress (ANC). Mandela forms the ANC Youth League (ANCYL) with Nick Gombart, Ashley Peter Mda, Oliver Tambo and Walter Sisulu. Mandela marries Evelyn Ntoko Mase, and they have four children.

1952
JUNE 26: The Campaign for the Defiance of Unjust Laws is launched by the ANC and the SA Indian Congress, with Mandela (by then president of the ANCYL) as volunteer-in-chief. Mandela is given a suspended sentence for contravening the Suppression of Communism Act (a wide-ranging act that included relatively small crimes including any activity that encouraged others to resist racial separation policies) and is forbidden to attend gatherings.

DECEMBER: Mandela and Tambo set up Johannesburg's first black law firm.

1953
Mandela and Sisulu begin discussing armed action and create the M-Plan. Mandela and Evelyn separate.

1955
Mandela meets a young social worker, Winnie Nomzamo Madikizela.

JUNE 26: Freedom Charter, a document created by the ANC, which among other things insists that 'the land shall be shared by all' and calling for the nationalisation of mines, is adopted.

1956
Mandela is arrested along with some 155 others; they are all charged with treason, arising from provisions in the Freedom Charter which the State tries to prove is Communist. Mandela, along with many leading ANC members charged in this Treason Trial, is banned for another five years.

1958
Mandela and Evelyn are divorced, and he and Winnie marry.

1960
MARCH 21: The Sharpeville Massacre sees 69 people killed after responding to protest calls organised by a breakaway faction of the ANC, the Pan Africanist Congress (PAC). The PAC and ANC are outlawed. Mandela, along with scores of others, is detained.

1961
The Treason Trial collapses and all are acquitted. Mandela goes into hiding.

DECEMBER 16: Launch of Umkhonto we Sizwe (MK), the ANC's armed wing, with Mandela as commander-in-chief.

1962
JANUARY: Mandela receives military training in Algeria and Ethiopia. On his return to South Africa, he is convicted of leaving the country illegally and inciting workers to strike.

1963
JULY 11: Mandela is in jail when police raid Liliesleaf farm in Rivonia, Johannesburg, and arrest the leaders of MK High Command. They are charged with sabotage.

1964
JUNE 12: After eight months of trial two men, Lionel Kantor and James Bernstein, are acquitted; Mandela, Sisulu, Ahmed Kathrada, Raymond Mhlaba, Andrew Mlangeni, Denis Goldberg, Elias Motsoaledi and Govan Mbeki are sentenced to life imprisonment. All of them, apart from Goldberg, who is white, are sent Robben Island.

1969

APRIL: Mandela writes to government calling for his release and that of his comrades or their recognition as political prisoners. He drafts a letter to government pointing out the lenient treatment of Boer rebels and Nazi-sympathising Afrikaners during the Second World War. Government, which included some of those former Nazi-sympathisers, ignores his missive.

1973

DECEMBER: Minister of Police Jimmy Kruger meets with Mandela and a group of Robben Island prisoners led by Mac Maharaj. Maharaj says Kruger came 'to find out whether there was scope among the political prisoners for a negotiating base with separate development as the underlying principle'. Kruger is told that there isn't.

1980

OCTOBER 1: Mandela appeals to the Supreme Court to prevent prison warders from listening to conversations between prisoners and their lawyers. Judge President HEP Watermeyer and Justice EM Groskopf reserve judgement.

1981

JANUARY: Ronald Reagan is elected president in the USA and begins 'constructive engagement toward SA'.

DECEMBER: SA forces kill more than 40 SA exiles and Lesotho nationals in Maseru, Lesotho. The target of their attack is MK leader Chris Hani. However, Hani escapes.

1982

President PW Botha meets Zambian president Kenneth Kaunda and hosts a second conference with business at the Carlton Hotel in Johannesburg to present a strategy to reform apartheid. His rallying call: 'Adapt or die'.

MARCH: Justice Minister Kobie Coetsee says government may consider releasing political prisoners. Some of the Rivonia Trialists (Mandela, Sisulu, Raymond Mhlaba and Andrew Mlangeni) are moved from Robben Island to Pollsmoor Prison in Cape Town.

1983

Minister of Prisons Louis le Grange visits Mandela and appoints Prison Chief Brigadier Aucamp as a go-between between him and government. The Prison Board calls prisoners before them to discuss political issues. Mandela issues a directive to prisoners to discuss only prison-related matters and to say: 'Send your political representatives to talk with our political representatives.'

MAY: ANC detonates a car bomb outside Air Force headquarters in Pretoria, killing 19 and injuring 215.

AUGUST: United Democratic Front is launched, embracing 600 anti-apartheid organisations.

SEPTEMBER 3: Riots break out in Sharpeville near Johannesburg as a tricameral constitution comes into effect allowing Indian and coloured people a limited say in government. Blacks are excluded.

1984

MAY: Mandela is allowed to have a contact visit with Winnie, who talks of touching her husband's hand for the first time in 21 years.

JUNE: Foreign Minister Pik Botha and Defence Minister Magnus Malan meet officials of Angola's government and demand closure of ANC military camps in that country (many camps were already heavily infiltrated with South African agents, who poisoned water or assassinated key figures).

SEPTEMBER: Complaints about Mandela's incarceration at Pollsmoor, heard before the United Nations Human Rights Commission, say Mandela is sharing a damp cell with five others, making it difficult for him to study.

NOVEMBER: Mandela separated from other prisoners and meets with government appointed negotiators including General Willemse, Justice Minister Kobie Coetsee, constitutional expert Fanie van der Merwe, National Intelligence Service (NIS) head Niel Barnard and Mike Louw, also of NIS.

1985

JANUARY 31: President PW Botha tells parliament he will release Mandela if he rejects violence. Mandela says government must reject violence first.

JULY 20: State of emergency declared in 36 black cities and towns; 1,000 people detained within a week.

AUGUST 15: Botha's disastrous Rubicon speech – government had promised reform would be high on the agenda, and instead Botha delivers a belligerent, blustering apologia for apartheid. The SA rand plummets. Academics, Afrikaans newspaper editors and businesspeople begin meeting with the ANC.

OCTOBER: Harry Oppenheimer, SA's wealthiest man, publicly supports the release of Mandela.

NOVEMBER 21: The ANC presents the Harare Declaration, its conditions for negotiations. It demands the release of Mandela and other political prisoners, the lifting of the state of emergency, the withdrawal of troops and repressive machinery from townships, the unbanning of the ANC and the creation of conditions for free political activity.

DECEMBER: Jay Naidoo, General Secretary of the newly formed Congress of SA Trade Unions (Cosatu), meets with the ANC in Harare. Government says it will talk to the ANC if it renounces violence. The ANC says government has to renounce violence too.

1986
JANUARY: Government hints that Mandela will be released in return for the release of jailed Soviet dissidents Anatoly Shcharansky and Andrei Sakharov. In the ANC policy statement of 8 January, ANC president Oliver Tambo incorporates a veiled message to Mandela: 'Our strength lies in our unity.' The ANC calls for a grand alliance against apartheid, incorporating businessmen, whites and opinion makers, to force government to the negotiating table by 1990.

FEBRUARY: In his opening of parliament address Botha says apartheid is outdated and commits his administration to moving away from it.

MARCH 16: Signing of the Nkomati Accord with Samora Machel, president of Mozambique, which pledges to have the ANC removed from Mozambican soil.

MARCH: Talks held in Harare between exiled ANC and Cosatu leaders Jay Naidoo, Sydney Mufamadi and Cyril Ramaphosa.

MAY: Commonwealth Eminent Persons Group gives government a proposal with a deadline: release Mandela, unban the ANC, declare a truce with the ANC, and begin negotiations. Government, faced with rightwing militancy, rejects this.

OCTOBER 2: Comprehensive Anti-Apartheid Act, sponsored by Representative William Gray of Pennsylvania and propelled by Senators Tom Harkin and Edward Kennedy becomes law against a presidential veto from Ronald Reagan. This law, which brings in wide-ranging sanctions against South Africa and massive disinvestment, becomes a global model. No other act is as effective in ending apartheid.

OCTOBER 19: President Samora Machel's aircraft crashes in SA, killing him and 38 others.

1987
JANUARY 8: ANC slogan becomes: 'Our goal is in sight'.

JULY: Institute for Democratic Alternative directors Alex Boraine and Frederik van Zyl Slabbert lead a group of business-people, academics, writers and poets to Dakar, Senegal, for talks with ANC leaders. The ANC moots two-sided negotiations, with the government and

its partners on one side and the allied 'forces of freedom' on the other.

AUGUST 13: President PW Botha instructs Justice Minister Kobie Coetsee to prepare the release of ANC Rivonia Trialist Govan Mbeki (77).

NOVEMBER 5: Mbeki is released after 24 years in prison but cannot be quoted nor is allowed outside Port Elizabeth.

1988
MAY: The ANC releases a draft constitution for SA. President PW Botha's bombastic ways cause increasing unhappiness among National Party (NP) leaders.

DECEMBER: Mandela is transferred to Victor Verster Prison in Paarl, where private meetings with government representatives are held.

1989
JANUARY 18: President Botha (73) suffers a mild stroke.

FEBRUARY 2: President Botha resigns as party leader; FW de Klerk is elected. De Klerk builds closer ties with moderate black leaders (Inkatha Freedom Party's Mangosuthu Buthelezi and Labour Party's Alan Hendrickse).

MAY: President Botha announces 6 September elections.

JULY 5: Mandela meets with outgoing president Botha at Tuynhuys, Cape Town.

SEPTEMBER: De Klerk is voted into power.

OCTOBER 15: The remaining Rivonia Trialists (Kathrada, Sisulu, Mhlaba,

Mlangeni and Motsoaledi) are released, but Mandela remains in jail.

1990

JANUARY 17: The Department of Justice says it is reviewing restrictions on all banned organisations, including the ANC and SA Communist Party.

FEBRUARY 2: De Klerk announces unbanning of all restricted political organisations.

FEBRUARY 11: Mandela is released. He returns to Soweto two days later.

APRIL: Matthews Phosa and Jacob Zuma lead initial ANC negotiations with South African government.

MAY 2–4: Government and ANC meet and hammer out Groote Schuur Minute.

AUGUST 6: The first agreement, the Pretoria Minute, on indemnity and return of ANC exiles and the release of political prisoners, is made.

1991

JANUARY 29: Mandela and Buthelezi have a failed meeting to discuss ways to find peace in KwaZulu-Natal.

APRIL 3: Mandela, addressing members of the US Congress in Cape Town, delivers a tirade against De Klerk about continuing violence.

APRIL 4: Mandela tells ANC National Executive Committee that he was wrong to call De Klerk a 'man of integrity'.

APRIL 5: The ANC delivers a publicised ultimatum to De Klerk: he has until

9 May to take seven steps to end violence or talks will cease.

JUNE: Mandela is elected ANC president as an ailing Oliver Tambo steps down.

JULY 19: Allegations are rife that the government is supplying Inkatha with guns and military training.

SEPTEMBER 14: National Peace Conference held in Johannesburg, first face-to-face meeting of Mandela, De Klerk and Buthelezi on one platform. Their unhappy faces in photographs display the mood – and act as portents for success of the meeting.

NOVEMBER 28-29: Sixty delegates from 20 parties lay the ground rules for multiparty talks. The Pan Africanist Congress walks out on the second day.

DECEMBER 20-21: The Convention for a Democratic SA (Codesa) begins with 18 delegations and government. Chief Buthelezi refuses to attend but sends delegates. De Klerk delivers a broadside against the ANC, and a furious Mandela lashes back.

1992

MARCH 17: After a major defeat in a by-election in Potchefstroom for the National Party, De Klerk calls for a referendum on his policies: 68,6% of the all-white voters show their support for negotiations.

APRIL 13: Mandela announces his separation from Winnie.

JUNE 17: Boipatong massacre, where 46 people are killed by Inkatha impi from

KwaMadala hostel. The ANC withdraws from talks.

SEPTEMBER 7: An ill-considered ANC/SACP march on Bisho, capital of the apartheid Bantustan of Ciskei, results in 29 dead and 200 injured as Ciskei troops open fire.

SEPTEMBER 26: Violence escalates nationwide; Mandela and De Klerk sign a Record of Understanding to get negotiations back on track.

NOVEMBER 16: Judge Richard Goldstone's commission (investigating misconduct in the police and military) raids Military Intelligence's covert operations centre resulting in the uncovering of data concerning state involvement in assassinations and violence. De Klerk appoints the Steyn Commission, which a month later suspends or retires 23 officers in what is felt is a damage control exercise.

1993

FEBRUARY 12: The ANC and government announce an agreement in principle on a five-year transitional period. During this time a government of national unity, which will be formed by the main election winners, will govern.

MARCH 5-6: Codesa talks resume as the delegates race toward a 1994 election, overcoming various obstacles including right-wing violence such as bombings and killings.

APRIL 1-2: Codesa holds its third plenary session with 25 parties participating, including the right-wing Conservative Party.

APRIL 10: Assassination of Chris Hani by a right-wing assassin.

APRIL 24: Oliver Tambo, president of the ANC from 1967 to 1991, dies of a stroke, aged 75.

1994
APRIL 27: At the age of 75, Mandela casts his first vote ever in South Africa's first democratic elections.

MAY 10: Mandela is inaugurated as South Africa's first black president with Thabo Mbeki and De Klerk as his deputies.

1996
Mandela and Winnie divorce.

1997
DECEMBER: Mandela steps down as president of the ANC.

1998
JULY 18: On his eightieth birthday Mandela marries Graça Machel, the widow of Mozambican president Samora Machel.

1999
MARCH 26: Mandela formally hands over the reins to his successor, Thabo Mbeki. Mandela is appointed mediator in Burundian civil war.

JUNE 2: South Africa's second democratic election is held. ANC president Thabo Mbeki is elected president of South Africa.

2001
MARCH 16: Mandela is awarded the International Gandhi Peace Prize, among dozens of honorary degrees and doctorates from various universities.

2002
FEBRUARY 10: Mandela is cleared of prostate cancer by his doctor.

FEBRUARY 17: Mandela creates a furore by criticising the AIDS denialist position of Thabo Mbeki's government's handling of the HIV and AIDS crisis. The following day the ANC National Executive Committee collectively rap Mandela over the knuckles for his outspoken stance.

JUNE: Mandela reiterates criticism on government's handling of HIV and AIDS at the 14th International AIDS Conference in Barcelona.

JULY: Mandela is awarded the Presidential Medal of Freedom, the highest US civilian award, by President George W Bush.

2003
FEBRUARY: Mandela criticises US President George W Bush for launching a war against Iraq.

MAY 11: Walter Sisulu, the man Mandela credits as his political mentor and closest friend, dies.

2004
JUNE: Mandela announces that he will be retiring from public life at the age of 85.

JULY: Mandela clashes with Mbeki about AIDS once more, and flies to Bangkok to speak at the 15th International AIDS Conference.

JULY 23: Johannesburg bestows its highest honour on Mandela by granting him the freedom of the city.

2005
JANUARY 6: Mandela's son, Makgatho Mandela, dies of AIDS.

2007
Mandela witnesses the installation of his grandson Mandla as chief of the Mvezo Traditional Council.

2008
JULY 18: Mandela celebrates his 90th year, and calls on the young to continue the fight for social justice.

2009
MAY 9: Mandela attends the inauguration of President Jacob Zuma and witnesses Zuma's first State of the Nation address.

JULY 18: Mandela turns 91. To celebrate 67 years of his service to the country, South Africans are asked to spend 67 minutes on this day to better the world around them; the day is dubbed Mandela Day.

NOVEMBER: The United Nations declares 18 July Nelson Mandela International Day.

2010
JUNE 11: Mandela's great-granddaughter Zenani is killed in a car accident.

2011
JULY 18: Mandela spends his 93rd birthday with family.

2012
JANUARY 8: The centenary of the ANC.

The first steps

We are not yet free, we have merely achieved the freedom to be free, the right not to be oppressed. We have not taken the final step on our journey, but the first step on a longer and even more difficult road. For to be free is not merely to cast off one's chains, but to live in a way that respects and enhances the freedom of others.

Nelson Mandela
Long Walk to Freedom, 1994

'THE PAST IS WITH US, not behind us. The traditions from which we come are in our words each and every day,' wrote African philosopher VY Mudimbe, and so to understand Nelson Mandela, it is fitting that we understand not only his earliest years, but some of the challenges society was facing.

Nelson Rolihlahla Mandela was born on 18 July 1918 in the small village of Mvezo in the Eastern Cape, in one of the most beautiful and isolated regions of South Africa. Although he was born of royal Thembu blood, the Great Place of the Thembu where he was raised by his uncle King Jongintaba is, even today, a modest compound: a cluster of homes and a single modern

house enfolded by steep mountains. In winter the hills are ablaze with vivid red-hot pokers. In summer the valleys are lush and green. Pink and purple cosmos cluster at roadsides. The Great Place is more humble than the home Mandela built in nearby Qunu after his release from 27 years in jail – a house that is a replica of the one in which Mandela spent his last years of incarceration at Victor Verster Prison in Paarl.

The youthful Mandela was imperious. He was a talented boxer and lawyer. He rose through the ranks of the African National Congress Youth League (ANCYL) in the early 1940s, pushing to the front of resistance marches. Two decades later he was among those battling to make effective bombs for the armed wing of the African National Congress (ANC), Umkhonto we Sizwe (MK), which he formed and led.

An impressive leader, he was but one of many exceptional black men and women who emerged and began discarding the chains of racism at that time. It was not necessarily apparent in the 1940s, 50s or even 60s that Mandela would become the

LEFT: Mandela was a keen amateur boxer in his youth.

OPPOSITE: Mandela wearing a beaded Thembu collar.

PREVIOUS PAGES: In 1952 Nelson Mandela and Oliver Tambo established the first black law practice in Johannesburg.

man of greatness he did. Certainly he was legendary in the 1950s and 60s, but, as anyone who lived through the resistance struggles of South Africa will tell you, there were many who were famed because of their leadership, bravery or compassion. They either died at the hands of the apartheid state, or were left behind by the course of events and subsided into relative obscurity; indeed, some died lonely deaths in poverty.

A young student teacher, who saw Mandela adjudicating a debate between the Jan Hofmeyr School of Social Work and the Bantu Natural College in Johannesburg in 1951, later commented: 'There was nothing striking about him, he was very judicial and very precise, careful in making judgements, he tried to make allowances.' Ten years later this teacher, Desmond Tutu, became a

ABOVE: Albert Luthuli, president of the ANC from 1952 to 1961 and 1960 Nobel Peace Prize winner, outside his house in Groutville, KwaZulu-Natal.

priest of the Anglican Church, and over the years grew to be one of the most beloved men in South Africa. In 1984 Tutu was awarded a Nobel Peace Prize. The same honour has been conferred on three other South Africans, two of whom were leaders of the ANC. ANC president Albert Luthuli received it in 1960; Mandela shared the prize with former State President Frederik Willem de Klerk, in 1993.

An early member of MK recalls that when Mandela visited London in 1961 and addressed a '... deep underground cell meeting to give us a briefing of what was happening in the country, he was confident, but we were not certain that his information was up to standard. It aroused some debate.'

Ben Turok, an ANC parliamentarian, politically active on the side of black rights since the 1940s, and in exile for many years, suggests: 'From the mid-80s Mandela became a symbol, but not because of his great leadership. The movement built him up. The movement decided "There's this guy, let's focus around him." We had no contact with him. [ANC president Oliver] Tambo had a bit of contact for a long time. The movement decided it needed a symbol; Mandela was the ideal hero of the struggle. It was decided: put him in the front line, campaign across the world for his release.'

In the end the prayers of a nation were more than answered when Mandela proved to be one of the most remarkable men the world has known.

The South African concept of *ubuntu* (a person is a person because of other people) is powerfully felt in the leadership of a competent politician, and it was exemplified in the tremendous humanity of Mandela. His story is more than that of just one person; without the exceptional courage of humble folk, who risk their lives and for whom no amount of bannings or persecution can end a desire for freedom and justice, no leaders can emerge to carry a cause forward.

Few other twentieth-century leaders, except, perhaps, for Mahatma Gandhi, whose life was also forged by South African racism and paternalism, has aroused such adoration from his people as Mandela. He and Gandhi united bitter foes by setting personal examples of their own humility and efforts to reconcile nations torn by bigotry and fear.

Although both saw reconciliation and negotiation as the way to heal their nations, neither was prepared to be cowed. Gandhi wrote that *satya* (truth) and *agraha* (firmness) '... engenders and serves as a synonym for force ... *satyagraha* [Gandhi's policy of nonviolent resistance] is not passive resistance'.

He insisted that it was '... cowardice to bend one's knee before an oppressor'. These beliefs had a powerful impact on Mandela and the ANC of the 1940s and 50s.

However, while *satyagraha* may have been effective against a government that would bow to pressure at home and internationally, such as the British Empire, it was ineffective against the barbarity of apartheid's governors, and so Mandela and his followers turned to armed resistance in 1961.

While Germany, shattered and humiliated after the Second World War, had the Marshall Plan to help it rebuild, Mandela gave South Africans important lessons in humility and compassion. South Africa, blessed without foreign intervention determining its future, would have to forge its own future; it will fall or succeed based on the success of its leadership and the determination of its citizens to work together and build their nation. Mandela's legacy was bestowing a sense of nationhood on a country deeply and deliberately divided. When he led as president, for the first time, South Africa's motto (Unity is Strength), adopted when it became a republic in 1961, finally meant something.

While Mandela's greatness was all-encompassing, it was the little ways in which he demonstrated humanity that touched a world starved of moral guidance. Derek Hanekom, who has served in every government since democracy, and as Minister of Land Affairs and Agriculture in Mandela's government said, 'Mandela is not always humble in private, but in public he has a way of approaching people and making them feel special. One of my staff wanted to meet him, and when she shook his hand she told him her cousin was a well-known sports personality. Mandela said to her: "Well, I will never again wash my hand, I am so honoured to have shaken yours". It meant so much to her.'

BELOW: South Africa was instrumental in forming the passionate resistance to racism and colonialism of Mahatma Gandhi (centre).

As another example, soon after his arrival in South Africa, before his credentials had been presented, James Joseph, the former ambassador for the United States to South Africa, found himself at an event with his wife. They wanted to have a photograph taken with President Mandela but were loath to intrude. Mandela, catching sight of them out of the corner of his eye, walked up to them. 'He held his hand out and said, "I would be most honoured if you would let me have my photograph taken with you",' Joseph remembers.

Dr Uwe Kaestner, former ambassador to South Africa for the Federal Republic of Germany, recalls Mandela's state visit to Germany in May 1996, when he addressed the *Bundestag* (parliament): 'After his speech, that was received with a standing ovation, he did not return to his seat but went straight to the leader of the Christian Democratic Party caucus, Dr Wolfgang Schäuble, who as a result of an assassination attempt is wheelchair bound. Mandela spontaneously greeted and embraced Dr Schäuble – in a gesture that certainly was not in any protocol programme.'

The capacity to empathise is one of Mandela's greatest attributes.

The South African constitution notes that South Africa is united in its diversity. But there is another area where many are united: in their love for Mandela. This book tells the story of a country's quest to be free, and of Mandela, just a man, a person because of other persons, and the greatest of all South Africans.

REPRESSION AND RESISTANCE

The men who formed the South African Native National Congress (later the ANC) in Bloemfontein were men of deep thought. Many were small farmers and businessmen frustrated that their labours were not rewarded as well as those of whites. They sat at their desks in publishing houses and stores and discussed the plight of Africans, and what other great revolutionary and pro-democratic visionaries like Thomas Jefferson, Descartes or Jean-Jacques Rousseau would have made of it. Govan Mbeki, one of Mandela's friends and comrades, wrote of how even in the 1940s and 1950s they sat on rolled-up overcoats in verdant valleys, blankets around their shoulders, and passed pipes filled with pungent tobacco, musing on how the 100-year Wars of Dispossession of the nineteenth century continued into the new century. They sat on cold concrete bunks with tin braziers spitting sparks of light into cold migrant workers' hostels, as they talked of the lands from which they had been forced, and the mines where they had to toil; they pondered what ways might be best for black people to regain their country, their pride and their birthright.

So, in 1912, they came to Bloemfontein by train and on bicycles, ox carts and foot to found the Native National Congress, two years after the Union of South Africa was formed and one year before the government instituted a process which led to the radical removal of land rights from African people. White colonists were unhappy with any African ownership of land. Through wars, and later laws, of dispossession, they pushed African folk into smaller and smaller rural areas, and introduced taxes to force them to seek work in the growing urban areas and mines.

These issues troubled the intellectuals of the Native National Congress, who attempted a discourse with government and opposition parties while building support among unionised workers. However, after the 1922 mineworkers' strike, when the red flag of socialism began waving at more rallies, the National Party government of Prime Minister James Barry Munnik Hertzog intervened to advantage white workers. His policy of divide and rule would form a cornerstone of National Party politics after that. The burgeoning multi-racial union movement began disintegrating and black unionism started to rise. White workers turned their backs on organised labour as successive governments clamped down on black unions and gave privileges to non-unionised white workers. These

Insult offered to a single innocent member of a nation is tantamount to insulting the nation as a whole. It will not, therefore, do to be hasty, impatient or angry. But God will come to our help, if we calmly think out and carry out in time measures of resistance, presenting a united front and bearing the hardship, which such resistance brings in its train.

Mahatma Gandhi
Satyagraha in South Africa, 1928

RIGHT: The ANC of the 1930s was led by the man whose vision saw it founded, Pixley kalsaka Seme. However, in the 1930s the group of intellectuals that led it failed to inspire and saw the ANC struggle to survive.

included certain categories of jobs being reserved for whites, and a prohibition on black people rising to any post where they might be in a position of authority over white workers.

Govan Mbeki, who was later jailed with Mandela, wrote: 'The decade 1936 to 1946 marked a departure from years of inactivity to a new phase in the struggle for liberation. The All-African Convention [AAC] had been convened for the specific purpose of marshalling Africans in every walk of life to fight the disenfranchisement of African voters in the Cape. But with the passing of the Representation of Natives Act in 1936 the AAC failed in its task.' This law placed black voters on a separate voters' roll in the Cape, the only place where they had been able to vote during the past 80 years.

Mandela was incensed, it was part of his motivation in founding the ANCYL in 1944 under the leadership of Anton Lembede. Mandela and his friends Oliver Tambo and Walter Sisulu rapidly rose to senior positions. They had already noted a pattern emerging between the State and its black subjects that would embed itself in South African political life: repression, resistance, severe repression and yet stronger resistance, which would over the years see those opposed to apartheid increasingly driven underground and into more militant subterfuge.

The length of the term of slavery depends largely on the oppressed themselves and not on the oppressor.

Chief Albert Luthuli
(President General of the ANC)
Presidential Address to 45th National Conference of the ANC, Orlando, December 1957

During my lifetime I have dedicated myself to this struggle of the African people. I have fought against white domination, and I have fought against black domination. I have cherished the ideal of a democratic and free society in which all persons live together in harmony and with equal opportunities. It is an ideal which I hope to live for and achieve. But if needs be, it is an ideal for which I am prepared to die.

Nelson Mandela
During his trial, 1963

RIGHT: People collecting signatures on 24 June 1955 for the adoption of the Freedom Charter. On 26 June the Congress of the People drew up the Freedom Charter at Kliptown, a village near Johannesburg.

THE M PLAN

In 1950, a string of annual events began, centring around 26 June: the ANC and South African Indian Congress (SAIC) declared a National Day of Protest and Mourning in the wake of 1949 riots between Africans and Indians in then Natal. Influenced by the non-violent protest actions advocated by Mahatma Gandhi, on 26 June 1952 the Campaign for the Defiance of Unjust Laws was launched by the ANC and the SAIC, and 8,400 volunteers went to jail for defying apartheid legislation. Mandela was volunteer-in-chief and Yusuf Cachalia, of the SAIC, his deputy.

Mandela and Tambo had only months before begun their law practice. The Transvaal Law Society immediately tried to have the sign 'Mandela and Tambo', on the second-floor window of Chancellor House near the Johannesburg Magistrates' Courts, removed. The society petitioned the Supreme Court to have Mandela struck off the attorneys' roll because of his role in the Defiance Campaign. They failed.

Mandela, realising the need for secrecy, devised the M Plan, which saw branches of the ANC divided into cells based on a single street; seven cells would make a zone, and four zones

OPPOSITE: Dr JS Moroka, Nelson Mandela and Yusuf Dadoo during the 1952 Defiance Campaign.

BELOW: Yusuf Dadoo, one of the most important Indian leaders of the South African resistance struggle, and Nelson Mandela surrender to the police during the Defiance Campaign.

RIGHT (TOP TO BOTTOM) (Treason Trial): Helen Joseph, one of the 156 Treason Trialists; Mandela arrives at the Old Drill Hall, Johannesburg, 1956; and Mandela speaks with his co-defendants outside the Treason Trial in the late 1950s.

OPPOSITE: Mandela stands out among his fellow accused in the centre of the third row.

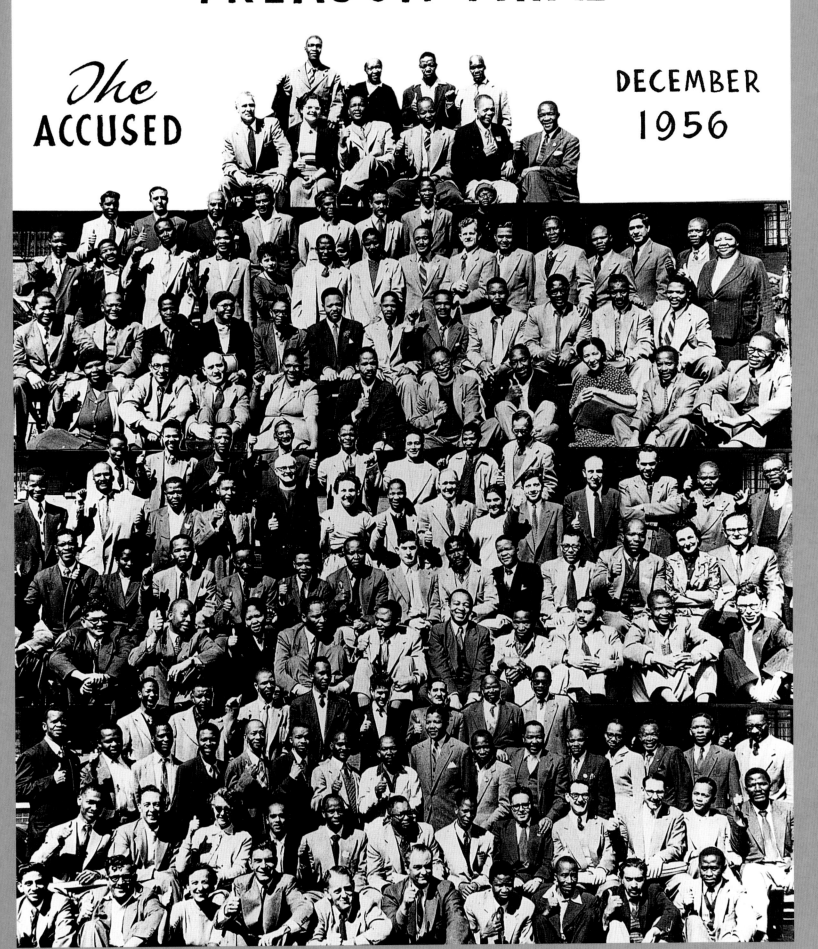

TREASON TRIAL

The ACCUSED

DECEMBER 1956

comprised one ward. This later formed the basis of the ANC's underground cell structure for political activists and MK. The M Plan was successfully used in the 1980s (though it was not known by this name) as street committees and block committees sprang up in every township to resist apartheid. Govan Mbeki later reflected, 'The government, by its repressive laws, kept pushing us deeper and deeper underground, honing our recruitment and actions, making us better and better.'

The M Plan was essential to all that was to follow. In 1953, Professor ZK Matthews, one of the ANC's most respected leaders, influenced by the Atlantic Charter and United States President Franklin D Roosevelt's *Four Freedoms* (freedom of speech and expression, freedom of worship, freedom from want and freedom from fear), suggested a Freedom Charter. That year, the national conference of the ANC called for the organisation of a Congress of the People. Convened at Kliptown, near Johannesburg, on 26 June 1955, the congress drew up the Freedom Charter – a declaration of basic principles honouring the rights of the most humble to equality and a share in the resources of a country wealthy in natural resources – it would become the ANC's seminal organisational and policy manifesto for almost four decades.

The Treason Trial began in 1956 and continued for four years. Among the 156 accused were Oliver Tambo, Nelson Mandela, Walter Sisulu, Ben Turok (who wrote the economic clause of the charter) and Helen Joseph. During the trial the State tried, and failed, to prove that the Freedom Charter was a communist document. Towards the end of March 1961, Mandela appeared at the All-in-Conference in Pietermaritzburg and called for a national convention before South Africa became a republic, as it was in the process of doing to release it from its colonial ties with Britain.

Mandela and the ANC organised a general strike for 29 to 31 May during which 10,000 people, mostly African, refused to go to work, but a massive police clampdown saw the strike faltering on the second day. Mandela devoted five pages of a 13-page report on the strike to lashing the press for its cowardice in failing to report accurately, as he saw it, on the build-up to the strike, and later publishing articles saying the strike had failed.

In its letter *Freedom Justice and Dignity*, released on 26 June 1961 from underground headquarters, the ANC said: 'A full scale

IF GOVERNMENT REFUSES NATIONAL CONVENTION...

ALL-IN CONFERENCE CALLS FOR ACTION

NEW AGE

Vol. 7. No. 24. Registered at the G.P.O. as a Newspaper   **6d.**
SOUTHERN EDITION   Thursday, March 30, 1961   **5c.**

Mass Demonstrations On Eve of Republic

Photos by Joe Gqabi and Bala Govender
and story from M. P. Naicker

MARITZBURG.

THE ALL AFRICAN PEOPLE'S CONFERENCE HELD AT PIETERMARITZBURG LAST SATURDAY WAS AN UNQUALIFIED SUCCESS.

Over 1,400 delegates attended and unanimously demanded . . .
● "that a National Convention of elected representatives of all adult men and women on an equal basis irrespective of race, colour, creed or other limitations be called not later than May 31, 1961."

The conference also resolved:
● "that should the minority Government ignore this demand of the united will of the African people . . .
1. To call on the people to organise mass demonstrations throughout the country on the eve of the declaration of the Republic on May 31.
2. To call on all Africans not to co-operate or collaborate with the proposed S.A. Republic or any other

form of Government which rests on force to perpetuate the tyranny of a minority; and, to organise and unite in town and country to carry out constant actions to oppose oppression and win freedom.

3. To call on the Indian and Coloured communities and all democratic Europeans to join forces with us in opposition to a regime which is bringing South Africa to disaster . . ."

The highlights of this magnificent Conference were . . .
● The patience and seriousness with which the delegates from all over South Africa met and discussed the problems that faced them. They conferred throughout Saturday night, even though many of them were tired after travelling the previous night in order to get to Conference . . .
● The inspiring opening address by Mr. Nelson Mandela, former President of the banned African National Congress (Transvaal), whose every sentence was either cheered or greeted with cries of "shame" when he referred to atrocities perpetrated against the people by the Nationalist Government.
● The representative character of the delegates, old and young, who had travelled many miles to be at Conference. There were delegates from Thogazi in Zululand; St. Faith's, near Port Shepstone; Ixopo, New Hanover, Tembuland, Pondoland, Zeerust and Sekhukhuneland. They came from New Brighton and Moroka, Alexandra and Langa. *(Continued on page 3)*

Mr. Nelson Mandela delivering his inspiring opening address to the Maritzburg conference.

AFRICA DAY SPECIAL

In commemoration of Africa Day (April 15), New Age will distribute FREE with each copy of the paper | published on Thursday, April 13, a portrait of Chief A. J. Lutuli. Order your copy now.

TREASON TRIAL MAY END THIS WEEK

JOHANNESBURG.

THERE WAS AN ELECTRIC ATMOSPHERE IN THE TREASON TRIAL COURT WHEN THE JUDGES ADJOURNED THE CASE LAST FRIDAY UNTIL WEDNESDAY OF THIS WEEK. IT LOOKED AS THOUGH AFTER FOUR AND A HALF YEARS OF PAINFUL NEVER-ENDING EVIDENCE AND ARGUMENT THE BIG CASE MIGHT SUDDENLY COLLAPSE.

The judges broke into the Defence argument when Advocate A. Fischer was on his feet arguing on the meetings the 28 accused had addressed. The presiding judge, Mr. Justice Rumpff, said the Bench thought it might shorten the proceedings if it interrupted the Defence argument and adjourned for six days for the judges to consider the legal points so far argued.

The Crown argument has lasted almost four months. The Defence has been arguing for three weeks. This is the second interruption of the Defence argument by the Bench. The first was to call on the Crown to answer the weighty legal arguments advanced by the Defence before its case was fully argued. This second adjournment was called for by the Bench after Mr. Trengove had already completed the Crown's reply to the Defence legal argument.

Abandoning the first hall, which had been wired by the Special Branch, the people marched two miles in the rain to another hall and countrywide campaign of non-cooperation with the government will be launched immediately ... we plan to make government impossible. Those who are voteless cannot be expected to continue paying taxes to a government which is not responsible to them ...'.

In January 1962 Mandela travelled to North and East Africa, as well as some European nations, where he met major African leaders, underwent military training with the Algerian army and briefly met MK members who had left the country to set up military units abroad.

Not long after his return to South Africa he was arrested and charged with leaving the country illegally and inciting workers to strike. He appeared in court with an animal hide draped across his shoulders; his wife Winnie wore traditional Xhosa dress. Mandela was displaying his stature as a royal African leader. It was a clever strategic act designed to assure traditional Africans that he spoke for them, while giving a Pan-Africanist message to more sophisticated opponents of racism.

Mandela in later statements talked of how important the ANC was to him when he said: 'The ANC's policy was one which appealed to my deepest inner convictions. It sought for the unity of all Africans, overriding tribal differences among them. It sought the acquisition of political power for Africans in the land of their birth ... I have always regarded myself in the first as an African patriot. ... Today I am attracted by the idea of a classless society.' The speeches were perhaps overly dramatic for the relative insignificance of the charges, but Mandela was speaking to history.

general strike

by NELSON MANDELA
(Secretary, National Action Council of South Africa)

A REPORT OF THE 3-DAY STRIKE IN SOUTH AFRICA (MAY 29, 30, 31, 1961)

ABOVE: A police clampdown saw the 1961 general strike fail, as documented in this 13-page report by Mandela.

LEFT: Mandela in 1962 at the Algerian military headquarters, where he received training while he was underground. During this period he was known as the 'Black Pimpernel'.

Golden Rules for a Good Congress Member. Lead – don't Order! Congress members must be close to the people and trusted by them. They must lead, not dictate to the people.

African National Congress Handbook, 1952 (price: one shilling)

LEFT: In 1962 Mandela left South Africa and visited other African countries. He also met political leaders in London. Here he is photographed outside Westminster Abbey.

On 11 July 1963 history knocked at the door of Liliesleaf Farm in Rivonia, north of Johannesburg. For two years or so, the ANC leadership had used this farm as a safe house. (They also used Kholvad House in downtown Johannesburg, which Gandhi had established for deep underground meetings, and many senior ANC officials including Ahmed Kathrada lived here. However, the police never succeeded in interrupting a significant meeting here.) All of the members of the MK High Command, barring Wilton Mkwayi, who would be detained later, were arrested at Liliesleaf.

A few months after this, Mandela was transferred from Robben Island, where he was serving his three-year sentence, to join his comrades in Pretoria Local Prison. He was charged in what was known as the Rivonia Trial (it was officially 'The State versus the National High Command and others'), on 156 counts.

The State was seeking the death sentence. It failed in this quest and instead the presiding judge sentenced the accused to life imprisonment. With the exception of one of the co-accused

(Denis Goldberg, who was white and thus served his sentence in Pretoria Central), the Rivonia Trialists, as they became known, were sent to Robben Island.

UMKHONTO WE SIZWE

According to its manifesto, 'Umkhonto we Sizwe will be at the front line of the people's defence. It will be the fighting arm of the people against the government and its policies of race oppression. It will be the striking force of the people for liberty, for rights and for their final liberation'.

In 1961, after the three-day general strike, Mandela wrote: 'Is it politically correct to continue preaching peace and non-violence when dealing with a government whose barbaric practices have brought so much suffering and misery to Africans?'

Govan Mbeki wrote: 'At a meeting of peasants during the Defiance Campaign, one aged man [argued] with typical down to earth peasant logic that Africans had lost the Wars of Dispossession because the weapons they used did not match those of the Boers or the British. According to him, unless that imbalance was corrected there was no point in embarking on a defiance of unjust laws. Any talk of nonviolence in conducting such a campaign was merely to tickle the Boers ("*Niyawa-nyubuza Amabhulu; Le ea oa Tsikinyetsa Ma Buru*"). Having said this, he took his old military coat which he had folded to sit on, shook the grass off, and moved away.'

Whether to take up arms or not was a decision that took the ANC seven years to reach. Mac Maharaj, former Minister of Transport, recalls: 'As far back as 1953 he [Mandela], together with comrade Walter Sisulu, began to explore the need for and the possibilities of the armed struggle. He expressed his view at a public meeting and was summoned to explain his actions before the National Executive Committee. He accepted the reprimand of his peers and his seniors. He never saw this dressing down as a personal affront. It helped hone his instincts for reading the moment and understanding the rules by which one strove to better shape the ANC to discharge its responsibilities.'

BELOW: Winnie Mandela in traditional Xhosa dress (centre) with Violet Weinberg (right) and well-wishers during the Rivonia Trial.

It was a difficult decision, and one that caused heated debate within the ANC's inner circles, but it was a decision that had popular approval. In his 1943 *Letters to a German Friend*, Albert Camus, a French resistance pamphleteer during the Second World War, described the difficulty of taking a similar decision. He said that the French Resistance's hesitation in making the decision to take up arms meant that '... we paid for it with humiliations and silences, with bitter experiences, with prison sentences, with executions at dawn, with desertions and separations, with daily pangs of hunger, with emaciated children and above all with humiliation of our human dignity ... It took us all that time to find out if

33

we had the right to kill men ... It taught us that the spirit is of no avail against the sword, but that the spirit together with the sword will always win the day over the sword alone ...'. These words could have been written by a member of the ANC, not only in the early 1960s, but until the day of democratic elections in 1994.

The laws which the National Party government rushed onto the statute books within the first two years of its 1948 election victory, and the harshness with which they dealt with voices of dissent, lent weight to the argument for an armed struggle. These laws made race an overwhelming determiner of whom South Africans could love and where they could live, attend school or seek work; they made humiliation the daily burden of the black South African, and opportunity the exclusive preserve of white people. The laws included the Prohibition of Mixed Marriages Act (1949), Immorality Amendment Act (1950), Population Registration Act (1950), Suppression of Communism Act (1950), Group Areas Act (1950), Natives Abolition of Passes and Co-Ordination of Documents Act (1952), Separate Amenities Act (1953) and Bantu Education Act (1953). These acts, and others like them, excluded black people from attending universities in white areas. They compelled black people, who formed 80 percent of the population, to live on 13 percent of the land – and the least arable land in the country at that.

During the early days of MK its leader Mandela knew nothing of warfare, of weapons, or of military strategy. The late Joe Slovo, a Johannesburg lawyer who would become MK chief of staff, recalled the first days in 1960 and 1961: 'Among the lot of us we did not have a single pistol. No-one we knew had ever engaged in urban sabotage with home made explosives. Jack Hodgson had been through the war, a veteran of the Abyssinian campaign and a full time leader of the [anti-fascist and anti-apartheid] Springbok Legion. Into Jack's and Rica's flat, sacks of permanganate of potash were brought and we spent days with mortars and pestles grinding this substance to a fine powder. After December 16 [1960] most homes were raided but not the Hodgsons'.'

This substance, more commonly used in washing lettuce, mixed with aluminium powder and catalysed by a drop of acid could make an effective explosion. For timing devices they experimented to find out how long it took the acid to eat through various thicknesses of cardboard.

With such a primitive mechanism, Slovo set out to burn down the Johannesburg Drill Hall, where the preparatory examination of the Treason Trial of 1956 was held. He entered the hall and found about 50 cleaners polishing the floors and wooden chairs. He put the bottle upside down behind a cupboard and then heard, 'Can I do anything for you, sir?'

Slovo, knowing there were a scant 15 minutes before the acid dripped through the potash and exploded, said his brother had received call-up papers but needed to take an exam. The officer asked Slovo to follow him. Fortunately the exemptions officer was not there, and Slovo was asked to come back another day. As soon as he could, he grabbed the tennis ball cylinder, which housed the ingredients, and defused the bomb.

The next day, he and his friends discovered that Petros Molefe had been killed near his target by a premature explosion. He was the first MK cadre to die in action.

The first test explosions of MK bombs took place at a disused brickworks. Mandela led this expedition, which launched Molotov cocktails against a wall. The next test involved placing a bomb in a pit. According to their calculations the bomb should have exploded in 15 minutes. When, after 25 minutes, it had still not exploded, a volunteer climbed into the pit and adjusted the bomb. He was barely out of the pit when there was a huge explosion. A number of blasts took place not long after that.

OPPOSITE: Yusuf Dadoo and Joe Slovo demonstrate in London for the Rivonia Trialists to be spared the noose.

RIGHT: In 1979 the ANC's highly disciplined Solomon Mahlangu Unit targeted the oil refineries of Sasol One and Sasol Two. These operations were among the most significant ANC military victories and saw no loss of life. This unit also hit several oil storage depots like the one depicted here.

In 1961, Joe Gqabi and Joe Modise, leading a unit to New Canada rail station at 3 a.m., took a stone, tied it to a wire and threw it across the line supplying the electricity. Modise recalled: 'We saw a blue flame coming out of the electric wire when the contact was made. We were sure there was going to be a short circuit but to our disappointment an hour later a train passed. Joe Gqabi then placed a stick of dynamite on the line and although it exploded the damage was minimal.' They later went to Mondeor, a Johannesburg suburb, almost rural in those days and sparsely populated, and destroyed telephone lines by tying a wire to the lines and pulling them down with the car.

Ebrahim Ismail Ebrahim was part of the Natal High Command along with Ronnie Kasrils, Billy Nair and Curnick Ndlovu (Bruno Mtolo, Mr X in the Rivonia Trial, who betrayed his former friends, was also a member). Ebrahim recalled his early training as '... crude, we only had dynamite which we stole; we had no revolvers or AKs, let alone knew how to use them'. The first time they stole dynamite they found little pieces with the explosive; they threw them away, only to learn later that they were the detonators.

At the twenty-fifth anniversary of the organisation in 1986, a time when detentions and repression were at their highest in South Africa, Oliver Tambo, commander-in-chief of MK, said: 'Our problem was not whether to fight but how to continue the fight. We of the ANC had always stood for a non-racial democracy and we shrank from any action, which might drive the races further apart than they already were. But fifty years of non-violence [before the formation of MK] had brought the African people nothing but more and more repressive legislation and fewer and fewer rights.'

Essentially MK remained a ragtag army, poorly resourced with increasing tendencies in the 1980s toward torture and repression of rogue elements, or those who were suspected by officials of being spies in its camps. The June 1976 uprising of Soweto youth against the Afrikaans language as a medium of instruction, largely motivated by the Black Consciousness Movement, transformed the thin guerrilla army. Thousands of young people left South Africa after police opened fire on marching pupils, killing 10-year-old Hector Petersen and many others. A firestorm whipped around the country, carrying talk of revolution and the beginning of the end of white rule.

The twenty-fifth anniversary issue of the MK journal *Dawn* noted: 'Almost overnight the Soweto generation enabled us to breach the barriers by which the enemy had sought to separate us from the masses.' Thousands of young people streamed across the borders to begin military training for the ANC and the Pan-Africanist Congress, which was opposed to white participation in the liberation struggle and even less prepared than MK. Highly motivated, bright and angry, they would change the lives of all they encountered – including their own. They entered an organisation that was ill prepared for such a huge influx.

By the time the ANC held its National Consultative Conference in Lusaka in 1985 (26 years after the last legal conference in South Africa) it was clear that the armed struggle was still seen by the ANC as the primary means of resistance: '... our armed units should be based among the masses of our people, relying on them for protection and sustenance, and, at the same time, drawing greater and greater numbers of our people into combat.'

BELOW: Electricity pylons were one of the first targets of the ANC's armed wing Umkhonto we Sizwe.

Love never gives up

Love is patient and kind; it is not jealous – or conceited or proud; love is not ill-mannered or selfish or irritable; love does not keep a record of wrongs; love is not happy with evil, but is happy with the truth. Love never gives up; and its faith, hope and patience never fail.

1 Corinthians 13
Read by Archbishop Desmond Tutu at the marriage of Nelson Mandela and Graça Machel, 18 July 1998

IN AFRICA, EVEN AN 80-YEAR-OLD MAN has to advise his chief when he marries. It matters not that he may be internationally famous, nor that he presides over the nation that the chief lives in. So it was that a fortnight after Nelson Mandela married Graça Sabine Machel, the former first lady of Mozambique, he travelled to his birthplace to ask forgiveness from the Thembu elders for not first seeking their approval. Some had voiced anger that he had not consulted them, but not all shared this disquiet; Congress of Traditional Leaders president Patekile Holomisa said Mandela's marriage on his birthday, 18 July 1998, revived an ancient practice: 'Sons of our chiefs used to marry daughters of other tribes. That brought peace between the tribes and consolidated their relations. So Mandela has symbolically strengthened relations between South Africa and Mozambique.'

Paramount Chief Buyilikwayo Dalindyebo, king of the Thembu and the son of Mandela's nephew, Sabata Dalindyebo, is four decades Mandela's junior. He also had no qualms about Mandela not abiding by custom. A modern king, Dalindyebo balances tradition with the norms and strictures of modernity. He has only one wife, although tradition allows him more: Mandela's father, Gadla Henry Mphakanyiswa, was a senior chief with four wives, his third wife, Nosekeni Fanny, was Mandela's mother.

Mandela had created a precedent when his uncle, Chief Jongintaba Dalindyebo, tried to arrange a marriage for him in 1940: the 22-year-old Mandela fled to Johannesburg. He was quite specific in the sort of woman he wanted to marry; it needed to be his choice and someone of intellect. When he met women he also sought the sweetness of his mother; he wanted someone that had her strength and resilience. He desired a woman with a strong sense of herself as an individual. He lost interest in one woman because she lacked this.

In Johannesburg, Mandela met a quiet, pretty girl four years his junior. Evelyn Ntoko Mase was a nurse with the Chamber of Mines and the daughter of a Transkei mineworker. She was supportive of Mandela's dreams of becoming a lawyer. He had studied toward a Bachelor of Arts degree at the rural university that had nurtured many African leaders – Fort Hare – which nestled in a somewhat ramshackle village in the eastern Cape, there he befriended a slight, bespectacled student – a fellow member of the Bible Society – called Oliver Tambo. Both were interested in the law as a career and a South Africa where skin colour would not be a determiner of success.

In Johannesburg, Walter Sisulu, who according to him, was with his two siblings born of the illicit union of a housemaid and the married wealthy building society boss she worked for in East London, had good connections in the white community. He helped secure a job for Mandela at the firm of Witkin, Sidelsky and Edelman.

PREVIOUS PAGES: Mandela arrives with Graça Machel for his 89th birthday celebrations, which he celebrated with children in Johannesburg, in 2007.

BELOW: A house at the Great Place of the Thembu, Eastern Cape, where Mandela lived as a boy.

Buoyed by the confidence of a steady income, Mandela and Mase married and quickly had three children; a fourth, a daughter, died as an infant. Evelyn became preoccupied with childrearing and her faith as a Jehovah's Witness, a religion that forbids political activity, and so the marriage experienced strains. In 1953 Mandela and Evelyn were estranged. Despite the intervention of Mandela's cousin, Kaizer Matanzima, the marriage could not be salvaged. Mandela made it clear to Evelyn that no attempt to save the nine-year marriage was worth the trouble – he had already met Winnie Nomzamo Madikizela – and so their divorce was granted in 1958.

On moving out of their Orlando West home Evelyn took their children Maki (2), Makgatho (5) and Thembi (8). She returned to the Transkei where she opened a general dealer's store. Thembi died in a car accident in 1969 while Mandela was in jail. The grief- and guilt-stricken father, because in truth Mandela had not been a good parent to the children born of his union with Mase, was not allowed to attend the funeral.

Evelyn, until her death in 2004, lived in a simple but comfortable home in rural Cofimvaba, the living room filled with photographs of her grandchildren. She had no bitterness about the divorce, and told those who asked that their marriage broke up because, 'Mandela wanted me to join politics and I wanted him to follow God.'

In 1955, Mandela met a 23-year-old girl with flawless skin, a ready laugh, and passions as strong as his. Winnie Nomzamo Madikizela seemed the perfect match and awakened in him an intense romantic love. The daughter of Columbus Madikizela, a prominent Eastern Cape tribal politician, she came from an important family, and was better suited to him than Evelyn, whose origins were humble. Winnie was the first black social-work student at Baragwanath Hospital and quickly became a close friend of Albertina Sisulu, the wife of his best friend. Here, at last, Nelson had found a woman passionate about politics and confident of her attributes. He found in Winnie a ready listener and supporter of his political views. She was astute in her judgements and was ready to respond to a political call to action, and with her beauty and rich deep voice, she was able to rally others too.

Winnie recalls that just over two years later he pulled up in his car and said, 'There is this woman, a dressmaker, you must go and see her, she is going to make your wedding gown. How many bridesmaids would you like?' They married on 14 June 1958. Zenani was born in February the next year and Zindzi followed in December 1960. Winnie better managed the balance between motherhood and political life than Evelyn's attempts to juggle her faith and children. Winnie also astonished Nelson with her stoicism and courage in the face of difficulties. He could not have chosen a better wife to keep his name alive when he disappeared from view on the Atlantic Ocean prison island, Robben Island, after his 1963 incarceration, but much was to happen before then.

Winnie's decades of suffering and police harassment started early, in 1959, when she was charged and then acquitted of taking part in marches. The ANC was banned in 1960 and Nelson went underground, becoming known as the Black Pimpernel. He received military training in Algeria and Ethiopia and visited a number of other African countries as well as Europe. In later interviews with me he spoke with affection, and some amusement, of this time. He was arrested and sentenced to three years in prison in 1962, and she was given the first of her many banning orders, restricting her to Johannesburg and her home from dusk to dawn. In 1963 he was charged and sentenced to life imprisonment with the other Rivonia Trialists.

With most of the ANC leadership in jail or exile, and channels like the International Defence and Aid Fund (IDAF) that would later pay for the education of generations of exiled children and the wives of imprisoned liberation struggle activists being established in London, Winnie battled financially. Amin Cajee employed her in his cobbler's shop in downtown Johannesburg, but security police surveillance and harassment was so intense that his business suffered, and she offered to leave. In later interviews she told me of her intense loneliness, of how others feared befriending her because of the regular raids on her home and the often visible police presence watching the movements of her and her visitors, the few that called.

Because of security police harassment she battled to hold down a job, until a photographic supply company, Frank & Hirsch, decided to ignore the harassment and employ her. They continued paying her even when, in 1977, she was banished to a small, dusty town in the heart of the country: Brandfort in the Free State.

Before then her life was lonely yet supported by excellent friends in Johannesburg. Her children often stayed with the family of Ama, Roy and Indres Naidoo or Helen Joseph, who scraped together their meagre resources to assist Winnie and the girls. Helen, in particular, a British-born anti-apartheid activist and who was childless, saw the girls as her own. Later, the IDAF helped send the girls to a fine boarding school in Swaziland, far enough away from the attentions of South African security police but close enough to visit Winnie occasionally.

OPPOSITE: Mandela and Winnie Nomzamo Madikizela on their wedding day, on 14 June 1958.

ABOVE: Nelson and Winnie Mandela –
their embraces were to be short-lived.

OPPOSITE: Winnie Mandela attending an
ANC Women's League rally in
Durban, 1990.

Nelson was allowed a visit from Zindzi in 1975 and had a contact visit with Zenani after her marriage at the end of the 1970s, but it was 21 long years before he and Winnie were allowed a contact visit. In the early years he was allowed only two visits a year, of half an hour each. They would speak into microphones and gaze at each other through narrow windows with thick glass. The visits were monitored, and if either said anything the authorities found unacceptable a screen would crash down, and future visits and the five precious letters allowed each year would be jeopardised.

Winnie was a favoured quarry of the security police; she was popular with journalists because of her beauty, wit and articulate views, and she was able to rally others to the ANC cause. On 12 May 1969, she was detained with 22 people under the 1967 Terrorism Act. When the police arrived, she was alone with Zenani and Zindzi, they were both younger than 10. The police were rough with the girls and refused to allow Winnie to call anyone to look after them. In an interview some years later, she told me: 'For 17 months I did not know what had happened to my girls. For me that was the worst torture.' In detention, she and many other women were kept naked, not given sanitary towels and not allowed to clean, so that menstrual blood caked on their legs. As she spoke of this time her eyes darkened and her voice lowered almost to a whisper; she said she befriended insects and longed for the opportunity to 'fight her way out of the cell'. The profound trauma of this experience never left her and may have formed the scar that determined later behaviour many would find erratic.

In 1991 Winnie said, 'I went through what everyone else did ... torture and detention,' but those almost-glib words disguised the horror of what she and thousands of South Africans experienced. The evidence of 12,500 applicants before the Truth and Reconciliation Commission (TRC) and the testimony of 7,500 victims told of torture, chemical and biological warfare against dissidents, disappearances, death and state harassment.

Archbishop Desmond Tutu, who chaired the TRC, on more than one occasion, put his head on the table he shared with other commissioners and wept as he heard how individuals were burned, mutilated and killed by South African security police. One of the most harrowing and well-attended hearings was the testimony as to how, in the 1980s, Winnie was involved in the murder of two young men, allegedly stabbing one, 13-year-old Stompie Seipei, twice in the throat before his body was disposed of by members of the so-called Mandela United Football Club. There is no doubt that the torture Winnie endured in 1969 and after never left her. Post-traumatic stress syndrome, common to people tortured or incarcerated, can be repressed for long periods but can cause violent or erratic behaviour when triggered by stress. Primo Levi, an Italian Jew interned at Auschwitz, wrote: 'Those who are tortured remain tortured ... gratuitous violence ... refuses to be forgotten.' It not only refuses to be forgotten, it sometimes fills the victims with a desire for revenge, and can cause deep psychological scarring.

I have often wondered whether any kind of commitment can ever be sufficient excuse for abandoning a young and inexperienced woman in a pitiless desert.

Nelson Mandela

RIGHT: Winnie Mandela during her banishment to Brandfort, 1977.

UNITED IN RESISTANCE

On 16 June 1976, Soweto school pupils, protesting Afrikaans as a medium of instruction, were shot at by police. Over the next few months thousands were wounded and more than 500 killed. Under the Black Consciousness Movement's Black Parents' Convention, Winnie and other parents came to the fore, and this saw her and dozens of others detained. Mandela applauded Winnie's decision to work with black organisations that had political ideologies different from the ANC. He indicated this in a speech smuggled to the ANC and which took two years to reach Lusaka: 'The first condition for victory is black unity. Every effort to divide the blacks, to woo and pit one black group against another, must be vigorously repulsed. Our people – African, coloured, Indian and democratic whites – must be united into a single massive and solid wall of resistance ... '. With this call, Mandela planted a seed in the ANC that led to the 1983 formation of the most successful legal resistance movement ever in South Africa, the United Democratic Front (UDF). It would later be renamed the Mass Democratic Movement and would be disbanded only after the unbanning of political organisations by President FW de Klerk.

I had hoped to build you a refuge, no matter how small, so that we would have a place for rest and sustenance before the arrival of the sad, dry days.

Nelson Mandela
In a letter written to Winnie from
Robben Island

But to get there pain and deaths would increase, and so Mandela intensified his call for united action, writing: 'The dead live on as martyrs in our hearts and minds, a reproach to our disunity and the host of shortcomings that accompany divisions among the oppressed, a spur to our efforts to close ranks, and a reminder that the freedom of our people is yet to be won.' To Winnie, he wrote passionate, sometimes lovesick, letters, commending her courage and initiative, yearning for her visits, and asking after their children. He would appeal to friends such as Helen Joseph to take care of Winnie. In return, they would send him news of his family. They also sent messages to him through other prisoners or communicated through coded messages via visitors. Robben Island had a highly effective smuggling network that saw such luxuries as precious radios and books occasionally making their way to prisoners past guards, but on occasion too, the friendships fostered with guards by people like Mandela enabled smuggling.

In May 1977, Winnie was banished to Brandfort, a dusty Free State village. Her house was tiny but had enough space for her later to build, with donations from American admirers, a small clinic, where she treated local people. Well-wishers in the United States sent her a beautiful

ABOVE: Mandela turned his Island cell into a home graced with a photograph of his wife and tomatoes from the garden that fellow prisoner Elias Motsoaledi lovingly cultivated from pips and smuggled seeds.

OPPOSITE: Winnie Madikizela-Mandela arrives for a TRC hearing in Johannesburg in 1997. The author can be seen in the background (holding a cellphone, seated right of centre).

handcrafted quilt, which dominated her small bedroom. Each day at 11 a.m. she waited at a public telephone at the post office for calls from around the world. Initially she was desperately lonely. Zindzi stayed with her for a while, but she had her own life to lead. Brandfort residents were divided between those who helped her and those who feared that kindness would lead to a visit from the security police. Her visitors were routinely arrested and some were jailed.

Nelson, in his letters, urged her to remain courageous: 'Had it not been for your visits, wonderful letters and your love, I would have fallen apart many years ago.' Foreign dignitaries and diplomats began visiting her, the most important of whom was United States senator Edward Kennedy, with a huge media contingent in tow, in 1985. The sense of compassion the American people had for her, and their generous financial gifts, would persist now and for decades to come, even as controversy dogged her.

No one in the ANC was as powerful as Winnie in drawing the press, or as skilful in playing them to her advantage.

In the end, however, the media turned on her. By the early 1980s reports were coming out of Brandfort of drunken brawls and affairs with younger men; the conservative black community was divided between disapproval and loyalty toward her. At first those on the left dismissed these claims as State disinformation, but investigations by ANC sympathisers showed many complaints and rumours to have substance. A conspiracy of silence began, with left-leaning journalists her most important protectors. When Winnie defied her banning order and returned to Johannesburg in 1984, it was a dream come true for the security police. She was becoming arrogant and unpredictable. Her romantic image began crumbling. The government hastened this by lifting her banning and banishment orders so that she could be freely quoted, and Winnie slowly became her own worst enemy.

Winnie returned to communities in upheaval; the townships were becoming war zones. In 1984, ANC supporters in Duduza accused a young woman, Maki Skosana, of being a police informer. Residents beat her and pushed her to the ground. Someone placed a tyre around her neck; others poured petrol over her. A match was lit. While her screams rent the air and bricks and rocks were thrown at her, she burned to death. That night her execution was shown on South African television and on screens across the world. One BBC cameraman was so upset after filming her macabre death that he refused to go into townships again and cover the violent unrest that had started engulfing the communities around Johannesburg and the eastern Cape in particular. Later, the TRC revealed she was innocent.

Throughout 1984 and 1985 dozens of government collaborators and police informers were executed by the so-called 'necklace' method first used on Maki Skosana. Some hardened media people could not bear to go into the townships, because of the gruesome sights they saw. On 8 January 1986, ANC president Oliver Tambo called for an end to necklacing. It stopped, but a month later, at a funeral for victims of police shootings in Mamelodi, Winnie lifted her fist before the crowd and said, 'With our matches and necklaces we will liberate South Africa.' Black South Africans argued over which call was more valid. The ANC in Lusaka was livid and told her to keep her mouth shut (a message which they would repeat more than once and which she would most often ignore) and to stop contradicting ANC policy. That year Mandela summoned Winnie to Cape Town where he berated her.

In 1986 the Mandela United Football Club (MUFC), which appears to have played no more than two matches in the five or so years of its existence, was formed. Its members were often seen travelling around Soweto or to political events in minibuses, the boys wearing tracksuits in ANC colours, Winnie accompanied them, dressed in military-style outfits. It was a year of fear in South Africa and perhaps the darkest year of apartheid brutality. In the course of that year, over 30,000 South Africans were detained by the security forces. More than 40 percent were children, some as young as eight. Three, aged 11, 13 and 15, died in police custody within nine days of their detention. Electric shocks were applied to the genitals, wrists, nipples and earlobes of children as young as ten.

From 1986 to 1987 I kept records of children detained for the Detainees' Parents' Support Committee. When I began volunteering at their offices in Khotso House (house of peace – which the security police would later bomb), 10-year-old Stompie Seipei had already been detained for some time. Occasionally I deleted names from the list, but Stompie's remained until media exposure forced his release. In 1989, a month after his body was found, after it was known that

Winnie had removed him from the manse of a Methodist minister, Paul Verryn (who later became a bishop of that church) I wrote in the *Los Angeles Times*, 'Stompie Seipei was a strong, brave little boy, far older than his years who saw one too many bodies shot in the street outside his home. He learned too many truths, too early.'

When Stompie's body was found, it showed signs of a savage beating; his throat was slit and punctured. In 1991 Winnie was convicted in Johannesburg's Supreme Court of kidnapping and being an accessory to assault in connection with the death of Seipei. Winnie was sentenced to six years in jail, which was later reduced, on appeal, to a R15,000 fine. In their 192-page judgement, the five Appeals Court judges in Bloemfontein, who were faced with the unenviable task of judging a woman married to the man likely to be the first democratic president of the nation in just a year, unanimously affirmed Judge Michael Stegmann's conviction of Winnie Mandela on charges of kidnaping four young black men in Soweto in December, 1988.

The Appeals Court set aside Mandela's convictions on lesser charges of being an accessory 'after the fact' to assault and reduced her six-year prison sentence to the fine and a two-year suspended sentence. It also ordered her to pay R5,000 (approximately $1,650 at the time) compensation to each of the three surviving victims. In December 1997, at Winnie's behest, the TRC conducted an open hearing into the allegations.

A poster on the wall read: 'Some of the crimes of our past: Murder, Abduction, Torture'. All were alleged in the two weeks of hearings into the activities of the MUFC and Winnie Madikizela-Mandela (a name she took after her divorce from Mandela). Evidence was heard about 19 deaths and 16 assaults, but it was clear there were more.

The final report of the TRC, issued in 1998, found 'Ms Winnie Madikizela Mandela politically and morally accountable for the gross violations of human rights committed by the MUFC'. The TRC found no evidence of Madikizela-Mandela's involvement in some of the killings that it believed may have involved MUFC members. However, it found that her vehicle was used in certain fatal 'operations', that she was involved in a number of kidnappings, and that assaults took place in the back room of her Orlando West home. Some of these she participated in, or knew of.

The TRC found that she took part in assaults against Phumlile Dlamini, and helped the killers of Phumlile's brother Thole 'evade the criminal justice system'. It found that Winnie was involved in the abduction of Lolo Sono, and that she 'must accept responsibility for the disappearance of Lolo Sono and Siboniso Tshabalala', both of whom were murdered by her associate Jerry Richardson – he would later be convicted of the crimes. She was also found 'responsible for the abduction [of Stompie Seipei] and negligent in that she failed to act responsibly in taking the necessary action to avert his death'. It further found that she was 'involved in and responsible for the attempted murder of [Lerotodi] Ikaneng', and that she was at 'the scene of the murder' of Maxwell Madondo.

He said to me that he was never so unhappy as in the period after he was released until he decided to leave Soweto.

Archbishop Desmond Tutu, 1998

OPPOSITE: Archbishop Tutu during Winnie Madikizela-Mandela's 1997 TRC hearings.

BELOW: Oliver Tambo (wearing sunglasses) with Samora Machel, the Mozambican president whose aircraft crashed on South African soil in suspicious circumstances in 1986.

The commission found that 'those who opposed Madikizela-Mandela and the MUFC, or dissented from them, were branded as informers, then hunted down and killed'. The TRC concluded: 'What is tragic is that so heroic a figure as Ms Madikizela-Mandela, with her own rich history of contribution to the struggle, became embroiled in a controversy that caused immeasurable damage to her reputation.'

Mandela was impassive during Winnie's 1991 trial and subsequent trials. He kept silent as newspapers recorded stores suing her for excessive, unpaid accounts and allegations of her abuse of ANC funds. As recently as 24 April 2003, she was found guilty on 43 counts of fraud and 25 of theft. Her broker, Addy Moolman, was convicted on 58 counts of fraud and 25 of theft. The conviction related to money taken from loan applicants' accounts for a funeral fund (common in African culture), but from which Moolman and Madikizela-Mandela said they did not benefit. Madikizela-Mandela was sentenced to five years in prison. Yet again, she appealed, but also, under pressure from ANC leadership, resigned her positions in the ANC, including her parliamentary seat and the presidency of the ANC Women's League.

In July 2004, an appeal judge of the Pretoria High Court ruled that 'the crimes were not committed for personal gain' and overturned the conviction for theft, but upheld the one for fraud, handing her a three year and six months suspended sentence.

Nelson Mandela was never tortured in jail, but he was severely wounded by these actions after his release. He had to endure the embarrassed shame of his colleagues who were unable to shield him now that he was free and no news could be kept from him.

Many reports of philandering had reached him in jail and just before his release Winnie's love letters to a young lover were published in a Sunday paper, as well as her threats to the mother of that lover's child. Mandela's wounds began to bleed, but he ignored them, believing 'love does not keep a record of wrongs'. It took him time to remember that love gives up when patience and trust, through prolonged abuse, fail.

On 13 April 1992 a visibly sad Mandela announced his separation from Winnie. With Oliver Tambo and Walter Sisulu at his side he falteringly read a statement at ANC headquarters at Shell House, Johannesburg: 'Her tenacity reinforced my personal respect, love and growing affection … My love for her remains undiminished.'

He told the divorce hearing in 1996, 'The bedroom is where a man and a woman discuss the most intimate things. There were so many things I wanted to discuss with her, but she never responded to my invitations. I was the loneliest man during the period that I stayed with her.'

ABOVE: In Graça Machel, Mandela found a healer of wounds, and South Africa gained a first lady who led by example.

OPPOSITE: American talk-show host Oprah Winfrey hugs her good friend Mandela.

I went to see him on one occasion when he had a knee operation … he was speaking on the phone to Graça in New York. He was beaming because he was talking to her on the phone. Teenagers have nothing on them.

Archbishop Desmond Tutu, 1998

Indeed, those who accompanied them on Mandela's first trip overseas, just three months after his release, in June 1991, told of how Winnie would berate and rebuke Mandela in front of his colleagues, profoundly embarassing him and them.

They had spent less than four years of their 34-year marriage together. Archbishop Desmond Tutu knew both since the 1950s; his Johannesburg home was a short walk from the Mandelas' in Orlando West. His face was sad and tired when he recalled, 'Nelson doted on Winnie. She has been a very powerful person and I want us to pay a tribute to her for what she stood for in those dark days when they wanted to destroy her. I would not easily condemn her. None of us can predict the pressure we can withstand. I'm still very fond of her.

'I got into trouble with the press when I said he is looking for someone to bring him his slippers. I meant he is looking for a relationship where he has someone who cares for him. He found her in Graça. She is a fabulous woman. She is all the things you want in a woman in many ways and is no doormat. I went to see him on one occasion after he had an operation on his knee. It was 11 a.m. and he was beaming because he was talking to her on the phone. Teenagers have nothing on them. She will remove a fleck off his shirt. I told him, "She really is very caring." He was delighted; he said, "Ah, you have noticed." Let me tell you, males are the most insecure people God created. And Mandela has found just the right sort of woman. When some people nominated her for the post of Secretary-General of the United Nations it was not a sop to her. She is one of the most highly motivated and intelligent women on this continent. Graça was Minister of Education in Mozambique and yet she so typifies her name. She is gracious. She is so solicitous of Leah [Archbishop Tutu's wife] and I when we visit. Their relationship is a gift from heaven for both.'

The first time Mandela reached out to Graça was in a message smuggled from prison after the death of her husband, Mozambican President Samora Machel, who died in a plane crash on South African soil in 1986. The crash, some have claimed, was probably caused by South African agents working with Mozambican dissidents to interfere with the aircraft's navigational equipment, but no proof of this was ever found.

Machel met Graça during Mozambique's long war for independence from the Portuguese. For the Front for the Liberation of Mozambique (Frelimo), which he helped lead, she helped set up schools in liberated territories and in their training camps in Tanzania. In 1974 she was appointed Deputy Director of the Frelimo Secondary School at Bagamoyo, Tanzania. When Frelimo formed an independent government in 1975, Graça, aged

LEFT: Few have done as much to combat HIV and AIDS in Africa, and South Africa, as US information technology magnate Bill Gates and his wife Melinda. Here they meet with Mandela and Graça Machel in 2003.

29, became a member of Frelimo's Central Committee and the Minister of Education and Culture. The only woman in the cabinet, she retained her post for 14 years.

In September 1975, she married Samora Machel, the first president of Mozambique, accepting as her own the four children from his marriage to his late wife. Samora and Graça had two children together.

Mandela was moved by the death of Machel, who had bravely supported the South African liberation struggle. This message, signed by Nelson and Winnie Mandela, but probably drafted by Winnie, displaying as it does, deep emotion, was broadcast on Maputo's radio station on 28 October 1986:

'We have never in our lives submitted a request to leave South Africa, but we believe that today we should be physically present near you. We are both detained in different jails. We have been prevented from being with you today to share your grief, to cry with you, to alleviate your sorrow, to tenderly embrace you. Our grief for the loss of Comrade Samora is so deep that it breaks our hearts. Throughout the night we shall join you in the vigil. Throughout the day we shall cry with you for the loss of that powerful soldier, courageous son and noble statesman. We must believe that his death will give new strength to your and our determination to someday be free. For you it will be through victory over the immoral and lackey bandits. For us it will be a victory over oppression. Our struggle has always been linked and together we shall emerge victorious.'

The relationship between Mandela and Graça Machel developed slowly after they met in 1990, when he went to Mozambique shortly after his release from prison. Oliver Tambo, who was ailing, had asked him to meet with Graça on his behalf. Samora Machel had asked Oliver Tambo to look after his wife and children if anything should happen to him. Tambo, weakened by a stroke, asked Mandela to take over the protective role.

Graça says frankly, 'It was not exactly love at first sight.' But over time they discovered that they had much in common. He invited her daughter Josina to live in his home in Johannesburg while she studied at the University of the Witwatersrand; their bonds became so close that Josina later wrote a book under the name, Josina Mandela. Graça describes Machel and Mandela as distinctive men, but with similar qualities. 'Sometimes when I listen to Nelson I even believe that it is Samora that speaks.' Graça muses that their shared experiences of pain added to their relationship: 'We enjoy this relationship with such fulfilment and such plenitude. It's so sweet and so complete and so normal. We know what the value is. We don't take it for granted. We know what it is to be without. We say to each other: "At last we are very lucky people because we could have ended up without being able to share this experience." '

The friendship of this strong, warm woman helped Mandela through the pain of his broken relationship with Winnie. Graça does not enter a room with the same drama and charm as Winnie, and is more low-key, but she too is tall, attractive and charismatic.

The couple have a strong commitment to the rights of children, and so it was natural that they should start the largest children's fund in South Africa. Graça is internationally known and respected for her United Nations-sponsored studies of the impact of war on children.

Her work with, and for, children received high recognition when, in 1994, then United Nations Secretary-General Boutros Boutros-Ghali appointed her to chair a study called the *Impact of Armed Conflict on Children*, the first of its kind.

She said during a keynote address in Pretoria in 1997: 'Gender-based violence is ... one of the world's most pressing issues and this same violence, directed against children during armed conflict, is its most horrible manifestation. ... Exposing children to atrocities, destroying homes, interferes with the development of a child's identity while often simultaneously robbing them of necessary parental guidance. We have to accept the responsibility that we have brought up a generation of youngsters who believe that to achieve something you have to use violence. Our children are becoming accustomed to, and are actively integrated into, this culture of violence. That's why we see gangs which are organised, banditry rising and hijacking and armed robberies mounting.

'In my country, it's much easier to get a gun than to buy a book for a child. The demilitarisation of society is a crucial factor in countering the culture of violence. Our armed forces have stopped making war but our societies remain heavily armed. Equally important is the need to disarm the population and demilitarise their minds to accept a peaceful way of relationships. We need to teach our children and youth that violence should never, but never again, be used to solve differences. Peaceful means, through dialogue and negotiations, is an issue that learning institutions from primary schools to universities need to address.'

On 18 July 1998, on Mandela's eightieth birthday and after a week of denying media speculation, Mandela married Graça, who was 28 years his junior. They had not even let their children into the secret, and after lunch had a brief and moving ceremony.

'Meanwhile,' Corinthians 13 concludes, 'these three remain: faith, hope and love; and the greatest of these is love.' Mandela and Graça Machel, who have retained faith and hope in a world that seemed determined to rob them of those qualities, have found the greatest gift of all in each other.

The influence of prison

Did I make the right decision in leaving my family and letting my children grow up without security? … Wounds that cannot be seen are more painful than those that can be seen.

Nelson Mandela

PREVIOUS PAGES: Table Bay and one of the most magnificent cities in the world, Cape Town, can be seen through broken walls from historic Robben Island. Views like this enticed prisoners like Nelson Mandela, reminding them of what they had lost and what they needed to regain.

OPPOSITE: Mandela burning his pass book in protest over the Sharpeville shootings.

BELOW: A mass funeral for the victims of the 1960 Sharpeville massacre. Demonstrating against pass laws, which required African people to carry pass books at all times, a peaceful crowd of several thousand people surrounded the police station at Sharpeville near Johannesburg. Panicking, the police force of 75 opened fire on them, killing 69 and wounding hundreds more. Most were shot in the back as they fled.

MANDELA'S CELL ON ROBBEN ISLAND was the colour of a jade sea under a stormy sky. It is little more than three paces wide and five long. Its high narrow window looks onto an exercise yard next to grape arbours, peach trees and flowers grown from pips and smuggled seeds. Visiting the prison in 1998, Mandela gazed into the cell where he spent two decades and mused, 'It seems so small now, but so big then.' And it was. He brought the universe into his cell: books, reflections on political debates, analyses of news broadcasts from smuggled radios, and snippets of news from contraband newspapers and journals.

Payment for smuggling was often made in diamonds – obtained by MK cadres from Angolan diggings or rivers – which were either given to warders or sold. 'One warder now has a beautiful house on Signal Hill in Cape Town,' reflected Mbeko Zwelakhe, a former MK soldier involved in smuggling operations, and who today runs a security company. The smuggling routes MK soldiers used persisted after the democratic elections in 1994 and even now are used to smuggle contraband, whether diamonds, stolen vehicles or drugs.

In prison Mandela learnt the lessons of survival: 'Prison is designed to break one's spirit and destroy one's resolve. To do this, the authorities attempt to exploit every weakness, demolish every initiative, negate all signs of individuality. Our survival depended on understanding what the authorities were attempting to do to us, and sharing that understanding with each other. It would be very hard, if not impossible, for one man alone to resist. But the authorities' greatest mistake was to keep us together, for together our determination was reinforced. We supported each other and gained strength from each other. Whatever we knew, whatever we learned, we shared and by sharing we multiplied whatever courage we had individually.'

In a letter to Tim Maharaj he wrote: 'It has been said a thousand and one times that what matters is not so much what happens to a person than the way such person takes it.'

Tokyo Sexwale, who later became the first premier of Gauteng, the richest province in South Africa, and, after that, a successful businessman, was jailed in the same section of the prison as Mandela. He says, 'There are four things you have to learn as a prisoner. First, there are the walls. You ... can see the walls and forever be a prisoner, or you can break through ... and have the whole world before you in your mind. The second challenge is the warders. Some were very harsh. Torture was not uncommon. But you had to work with them every day, and it might take years, but you had to turn them and change them, because they would become important for smuggling. ... The third challenge is your friends and comrades. You live at very close quarters with people you may have worked with outside, but living so close together under such difficult conditions brings out the best and worst in people. Some people you were very close to outside are impossible to live with in prison. And the fourth, and greatest, challenge is yourself. The enemy within. You have to work with and change yourself.'

Mandela said the enemy within makes you ask, 'Did I make the right decision in leaving my family and letting my children grow up without security?

ABOVE: In 1966, a reporter and a photographer from the *Daily Telegraph* in London visited Robben Island to satisfy the outside world that the Rivonia Trialists were not being mistreated. In this photograph taken during that visit, the prisoners on the left are breaking stones into gravel for Island roads. Those on the right are sewing mailbags.

Although I agonised over my family, I was still convinced that even if I had known how serious the consequence of my acts [would be] I would have done the same.' That realisation did not ease a sense of guilt and sadness. His mother died while he was in prison and he was refused permission to bury her. 'The next shattering experience was the death of my eldest son in a car accident. ... He was not just a son but a friend. The warders used psychological persecution – whenever something happened to my family, I would come from the quarry and find a newspaper cutting on my desk.'

Before prison Mandela tended to arrogance. Prison hardship taught him patience; the denial of rights – stoicism; learning of the hardship of others less privileged than himself – compassion and respect to the humble. He learned that education does not always form wisdom; experience can be a far better teacher. Prison made him one of the great leaders of history.

In April 1969, Mandela embarked upon the first of many initiatives over almost 15 years to begin talks with government. He wrote asking for his release and that of his comrades, or their recognition as political prisoners. He pointed to the lenient treatment meted out to Boer rebels and Nazi-sympathising Afrikaners in World War II by the British colonial power. Government ignored his missive.

Maintaining a rigorous schedule of meetings, talks and discussion seminars, he refused to allow his spirit to be imprisoned. Accepting India's Jawaharlal Nehru Award in 1980 (granted to individuals 'for their outstanding contribution to the promotion of international understanding, goodwill and friendship among people of the world'), he wrote a letter that was smuggled to the Indian government from his cell on the island. Quoting Nehru, he said: 'Walls and dangerous companions ... make you a prisoner and a slave ... [but] the most terrible of walls are the walls ... in the mind, which prevent you from discarding an evil tradition simply because it is old, and from accepting a new thought because it is novel.'

The letter gave insights into how prison formed his thinking: 'The politically inclined youth of my generation were drawn together by feelings of an intense, but narrow form of nationalism. ... Time was to teach us as Panditji [Nehru] says, that "nationalism is good in its place, but is an unreliable friend and an unsafe historian. It binds us to many happenings and sometimes distorts the truth."'

This underscored his presidency: he would bend to catch the whispers of a child, place a caring hand on the shoulder of an old woman. He even travelled thousands of miles to a tiny isolated village built for whites only, in a racist attempt at a white homeland, called Orania, to see Betsie Verwoerd, widow of the architect of apartheid, Hendrik Verwoerd. When he spoke to the frail old woman who had made hating black people her life's mission, he showed tenderness and courtesy. He bent close to her lips, lest he miss a word. The way she glowed in his presence was testimony that his journey was worth it. With this single journey across the country to a community as isolated from the nation as their ideology, he sowed division among the right wing; those determined to hate felt uncomfortable and confused.

Mosiuoa Patrick 'Terror' Lekota, ANC chairperson and Minister of Defence in the cabinet of President Thabo Mbeki, was also incarcerated on the island. He said, 'Prison compels a breadth of your vision and understanding. If you wanted something you had to get on your knees and plead with someone. This compels you to a sense of God, of you not being in total control of everything. There is a recognition that sometimes you have to depend on some other force, real or imagined. Anyone who goes to jail and is subject to those conditions learns humility. Prison tempered a lot of the animal instincts in us. Prison and age. You mix with people you never would have if you had not gone to jail. You share the same ablution facilities, eat the same porridge from the same plate, share the same blankets, you talk to people and discover that although they are not from the same social background they have much to offer.' Lekota ultimately left the ANC, angry with the way Thabo Mbeki was ousted as president in 2008. He formed an opposition party, the Congress of the People (COPE) that year but it never gained momentum because of constant bickering – the lessons learned in prison had been lost.

Mandela learnt in prison that the humblest people can sometimes have the greatest insights. Mac Maharaj, who was Minister of Transport in Mandela's government before being sidelined in 1999 by Mbeki, who feared him as a rival for the presidency, said Mandela's 'genius was that

ABOVE: Mandela and his elder son, Madiba Thembekile (Thembi), who died in a road accident at the age of 25, while Mandela was on the island.

he gave leadership to a disparate body of prisoners to act in concert to improve prison conditions. But he never made prison conditions the sole reason for any interaction as there was always a greater political purpose. Madiba also conducted himself in such a way that the authorities could never have the excuse to close the door on him.'

This was how he achieved a negotiated settlement for South Africa. It is clear that some in the National Party had believed that they could corral the ANC by unbanning it and allowing free political activity. At the same time elements in the apartheid government promoted State death squads, gun-running and the provocation of massive violence in black areas to force, so they hoped, black people to long for the firm leadership of the National Party – or the quiet of apartheid. By the same token, chaos was supposed to affirm to white people and to the international community that black South Africans were incapable of ruling South Africa and, left to their own devices, that they would cause the genocidal mayhem that has been seen in other parts of Africa. It's worth looking back at history a little to understand this thinking.

GOD'S SWORD

Mandela, with his willingness to talk to his enemies, subverted the plans of some in the white minority government who believed war and conflict would give it the upper hand.

One of the men who was central to the decision to release Mandela, and in the talks leading to the unbanning of the ANC, was Lukas Daniël (Niel) Barnard, a former professor in the Political Science Department at the University of the Orange Free State. His views were a perfect fit for the new government of Pieter Willem Botha who, in 1979, succeeded Balthazar John Vorster as president. Vorster's government had not seen the 16 June 1976 Soweto student uprising coming, despite Zulu leader Mangosuthu Buthelezi's eerie prophecy precisely three months before the uprising that 'South Africa is approaching its hour of crisis'.

PW Botha, while promising reform, handpicked as head of the National Intelligence Service (NIS) 31-year-old Barnard, making him the youngest spymaster in South Africa's history.

Barnard regaled journalists with his writings, which were peppered with biblical allusions to 'the sword of God' – in Afrikaans, military power is often referred to as *swaardmag* (sword power). He wrote: 'In world politics fragmented by sin, the sword must always be applied

justifiably for the punishment of evil. The attitude that the Christian state must never take up the sword and suffer for justice, is dangerous cowardice.'

South Africa began launching raids against its neighbours (Lesotho, Botswana, Swaziland, Mozambique, Zambia and Zimbabwe), purportedly against ANC guerrillas, but killing anyone in their way. In one raid at Matola in 1981, 13 ANC members were executed by South African soldiers wearing swastika-emblazoned helmets. The ears of the dead soldiers were cut off and taken back to South Africa as trophies for the attackers' commanders. Under Barnard and those

ABOVE: Robben Island, where Nelson Mandela was incarcerated for more than two decades until 1982, with Table Mountain in the background. The prison is located in the middle of the left side of the Island.

of his ilk in the military security establishment, death squads emerged and South Africa's chemical and biological warfare programme was honed. These squads developed poisoned T-shirts, anthrax-tipped cigarettes, and tear gas made out of marijuana, ecstasy and LSD.

Shortly before Mandela's release in 1990 some in the military establishment plotted to murder him with an untraceable compound that would destroy brain cells; it is a tribute to De Klerk that this merciless scheme was never implemented. But it was with these people that Mandela would need to later negotiate.

Hatred between those who resisted apartheid and the heart of the Afrikaner establishment blazed in the early 1980s. In May 1983, the heart of Afrikanerdom and the soul of whites were shaken by a car bomb explosion outside Air Force headquarters in Pretoria at rush hour. The blast killed 19 and injured 215. The impact on the ruling elite in South Africa was a little like that of the terrorist attack on the United States on 11 September 2001.

Police cordoned off the area as black smoke billowed above the city and radio stations interrupted all programmes. At the HF Verwoerd Hospital, dazed relatives wandered the hallways clutching each other and sobbing as wave after wave of ambulances screeched to a halt at the casualty entrance. This was an alarm that South Africa heeded – though it made many whites more belligerent. The ANC, which had earlier launched a rocket attack against Voortrekkerhoogte military base and the Sasol oil refineries, said it would remain focused on military targets but in instances civilian casualties would result. It was a clarion call to increased conflict and resistance that initially grew under the yellow, red and black banners of the United Democratic Front (UDF). Launched that August, the UDF embraced 600 anti-apartheid organisations, many with mostly white members.

PW Botha's reform initiatives, balanced with increasing repression, had yet to impress the international community, and the release of Mandela was becoming essential to real progress. In March 1984, over 4,000 foreign celebrities signed a petition calling for his release. Government ignored it and went on trying to root out ANC bases from what they called the Frontline States (Mozambique, Angola, Zimbabwe, Zambia, Tanzania, Swaziland and Lesotho).

In September 1983, complaints about Mandela's incarceration at Pollsmoor came before the United Nations Human Rights Commission (UNHRC). Testimony was given that Mandela shared a damp cell with five other prisoners, which made it difficult for him to study. Two months later, apparently in response to the UNHRC hearing, but more likely to promote the secret talks process, Mandela was separated from the other prisoners. Mandela recalls, 'I thought I should approach the government and ask for a meeting between government and the ANC – because we are products of a collective leadership. I agonised over the fact that I would approach the government without discussing the matter with my colleagues, comrades Sisulu, Kathrada, Mlangeni ... but I felt that if I did they would reject my move, because of our hatred of NP politicians. However, I thought the time was right for negotiations. My comrades did not have the advantages I had of brushing shoulders with the VIPs that came to prison, judges, the Minister of Justice, the Commissioner of Prisons.

'I decided to confront my colleagues with a *fait accompli*, so I approached the government and had discussions over some time with Mr Kobie Coetsee, who said discussions must be secret. I said confidential yes, but secret no. I reached a stage where I wanted to see my four comrades who were with me in Pollsmoor. The authorities refused and said see them one by one, so I called ... comrade Walter Sisulu. I calculated that if I convinced him he would help me convince the rest. He ... said Madiba, I have nothing against negotiations, but I would prefer that they start

We have set out on a quest for true humanity, and somewhere on the distant horizon we can see the glittering prize. Let us march forth with courage and determination, drawing strength from our common plight and our brotherhood. In time we shall bestow upon South Africa the greatest gift possible – a more human face.

Steven Bantu Biko
(Black Consciousness leader murdered by police while in detention),
September 1977

OPPOSITE: The late Archbishop Trevor Huddleston (centre) leads a prayer vigil in London.

first, not us. I said Comrade Tshepo [which means hope] if you are not against negotiations, it doesn't matter who starts. Raymond Mhlaba said, what were you waiting for all this time, you should have done this long ago. Comrade Kathrada said he disagreed with me. Comrade Mlangeni agreed.

'Then I smuggled a letter to the leadership outside. A reply came back from Oliver Tambo, there was a note of disapproval, he said what are you discussing with these fellows? I said, I am discussing a meeting with the ANC and government, just one line. I told them later in a memo that I was discussing violence, negotiations, the alliance with the SACP [South African Communist Party], the question of majority rule. The ANC said it was the right thing to do and authorised me. Then I called comrades from Natal, the Transvaal, the Orange Free State and the Cape, members of the ANC, the Youth League, the Women's League and members of trade

unions. I briefed them and no-one said no, I called the prisoners [the remaining Rivonia Trialists] from Robben Island too.

'The government appointed a top level team of negotiators: General Willie Willemse, Kobie Coetsee, Niel Barnard, then head of the National Intelligence Service, constitutional expert Fanie van der Merwe and Mike Louw of NIS. Then I saw PW in mid-1989. It was one of the best meetings I have ever had, he received me very well. I was removed from Pollsmoor to Victor Verster. Those were the best days in prison, because it was a stage between prison and freedom.'

General Willemse, who became Commissioner of Prisons in 1983 and who had known Mandela since 1971 while he was commanding officer on the island, said the meetings took place at Pollsmoor in VIP guest houses, in the VIP dining room, in the clubhouse, and once in General

Willemse's home within Pollsmoor precincts. Other meetings occurred at the home of Kobie Coetsee – he and Mandela once even played tennis – and at Victor Verster Prison.

The environment of the prison at that time was relatively tranquil compared to the fear and violence starting to prevail in South Africa. On 20 July 1985 a State of Emergency was declared in 36 black urban areas. In the first week 1,000 people were detained. On 15 August the world media cleared their airwaves for a speech from the president which government said would introduce radical reforms. Instead, in his 'Rubicon' speech, Botha delivered a belligerent, blustering apologia for apartheid.

Within days the currency dropped to almost a third of its value. Academics, newspaper

ABOVE: Bobbies restrain anti-apartheid protestors where the Springbok rugby team was to play in England, 1969.

editors and businesspeople became desperate; they decided that if government could not and would not negotiate a way out of the impasse threatening South Africa, they would, and so they began meeting with the ANC, despite government threats to seize their passports.

Harry Oppenheimer, South Africa's wealthiest man, publicly came out in support of Mandela's release. On 21 November 1985, the ANC stepped up the pressure by presenting their conditions for negotiations in the Harare Declaration. This document demanded the release of Mandela and other political prisoners, the lifting of the State of Emergency, the withdrawal of troops from townships, the unbanning of the ANC and the creation of conditions for free political activity.

Publicly the government said it would talk with the ANC only if it renounced violence; the ANC responded by saying government also had to renounce violence.

Mac Maharaj mused: 'We brought democracy to our country, but not within the textbook theory of revolution that we had cut our teeth on politically in the 1950s. The world had fundamentally changed by the mid-1980s. But whatever the changes are, history writes down as its leaders the men and women who have both the ability to detect its shifts and the courage to act on it. This is a measure of the leadership of Mandela, who decided in the isolation of his prison cell to take the initiative and open dialogue with the hated apartheid regime. ... History

RIGHT: The words '*liberté, égalité, fraternité*' from the French Revolution underscore the France of today and have influenced global thinking on democracy, as this anti-apartheid demonstration calling for the release of Mandela in Paris, 1986, reveals.

will record that Madiba ... read the moment correctly. ... Every lonely step he took to set up the preconditions for talks with the apartheid regime was carefully weighed to ensure he did not in any way undermine or compromise the ANC, and that any possible failure in his bold strategy would be borne by him alone without bringing embarrassment to his organisation.'

The 'securocrats', as the military and security police under PW Botha were known, developed 'total onslaught' and 'total strategy' claims for the threats that they perceived to be facing South Africa in the early 1980s. These justified, they said, a complex military and security police system that, as in Nazi Germany, encouraged citizens to spy on each other.

The State Security Council (SSC), which had been put in place in 1972 under the presidency of John Vorster, became the real government. The committee was one of 20 cabinet committees until 1979.

When PW Botha, who had been defence chief since 1966, became Prime Minister in 1978, he needed to assert control over the powerful Bureau for State Security under General Hendrik van den Bergh, a confidant of Vorster. Botha's sympathies lay with the military, the intelligence arm of which despised BOSS.

Since its 1975 invasion of Angola, the military had been at variance with cabinet. Botha and the military wanted to take the war to the enemy. Botha prepared the ground for harsh action against black citizens when he told the public that revolution was a possibility. He and his generals characterised anti-apartheid activity as a 'total onslaught' that only a 'total strategy' could confront.

Barnard wrote in the press, in words similar to those from the United States Homeland Security system after the 11 September 2001 attacks in that country: 'Terror is drama ... directed at the greatest possible number of people that can see and hear; definitely not at the greatest number of people that can be killed. To this end, the TV, radio and press is of great assistance to terrorism in the announcement of terror capabilities on the one hand, and the creation of sympathetic public opinion on the other.' Mandela's contact with government intensified in July 1984, when Justice Minister Kobie Coetsee visited him in a Cape Town hospital, where he was recovering from an illness.

On 31 January 1985, PW Botha announced to the House of Assembly: 'The government is willing to consider Mr Mandela's release in the Republic of South Africa on condition that Mr Mandela gives a commitment that he will not make himself guilty of planning, instigating or

RIGHT: Rivonia Trialists (from left) Denis Goldberg, Andrew Mlangeni, Nelson Mandela, Ahmed Kathrada, Walter Sisulu and Wilton Mkwayi visit Robben Island on 11 February 1994.

committing acts of violence for the furtherance of political objectives, but will conduct himself in such a way that he will not again have to be arrested ... It is therefore not the South African government which now stands in the way of Mr Mandela's freedom. It is he himself. The choice is his. All that is required of him now is that he should unconditionally reject violence as a political instrument. This is, after all, a norm which is respected in all civilised countries of the world.'

His genius was that he gave leadership to a disparate body of prisoners to act in concert to improve prison conditions. But he never made prison conditions the sole reason for any interaction as there was always a greater political purpose. Madiba also conducted himself in such a way that the authorities could never have the excuse to close the door on him.

Mac Maharaj

RIGHT: Mandela, two months before he was elected President in April 1994, stares pensively out of the high window of the Robben Island cell in which he was held for two decades.

ABOVE: The 'Groot Krokodil' (big crocodile) was the nickname given to President PW Botha, under whose watch death squads flourished and anti-apartheid resistance was fiercely crushed. He and Mandela developed a cordial relationship, as shown at this meeting in 1997.

On 8 February Winnie Mandela visited her husband with his lawyer Ismail Ayob to obtain a reply to the president's offer. Mandela chose to speak to President Botha through a public statement. While Ayob and Winnie sat before him, he began to dictate a speech, but a prison warder stopped him. Mandela said he had the right to reply to the president in whatever way he chose. A senior officer then appeared and told Mandela to desist. Mandela told the prison authorities to telephone the president. He then turned his back on them and continued dictating to Ayob.

On Sunday, 10 February, his youngest daughter Zindzi read her father's statement on a sweltering summer's day at the Jabulani Stadium in Soweto. The occasion had been planned by the UDF to celebrate the Nobel Peace Prize that had been awarded to Anglican Bishop Desmond Tutu in Oslo two months previously. Standing before the hushed crowd, Zindzi, dressed in jeans and a T-shirt, read: 'My father and his comrades ... are clear that they are accountable to you and to you alone. And that you should hear their views directly and not through others. He speaks for all those in jail for their opposition to apartheid, for all those who are banished, for all those who are in exile, for all those who suffer under apartheid, for all those who are opponents of apartheid and for all those who are oppressed and exploited ...

'He says, "I will remain a member of the African National Congress until the day I die. Oliver Tambo is much more than a brother to me. He is my dearest friend and comrade for nearly fifty years. If there is any one among you who cherishes my freedom, Oliver Tambo cherishes it more ... there is no difference between his views and mine ..."'

This too was also a clear message to those among the crowds who felt that Mandela might be speaking without the authority of the ANC in exile.

Zindzi continued reading: 'Let Botha ... renounce violence. Let him say that he will dismantle apartheid. Let him unban the people's organisation, the African National Congress. Let him free all who have been imprisoned, banished or exiled for their opposition to apartheid. Let him guarantee free political activity so that the people may decide who will govern them.

'I cherish my own freedom dearly but I care even more for your freedom ... I cannot sell my birthright, nor am I prepared to sell the birthright of the people to be free. ... What freedom am I being offered while the organisation of the people remains banned? What freedom am I being offered when I may be arrested on a pass offence? What freedom am I being offered to live my life as a family with my dear wife who remains in banishment in Brandfort? What freedom am I being offered when I need a stamp in my pass to seek work? What freedom am I being offered when my very South African citizenship is not respected? Only free men can negotiate. Prisoners cannot enter into contracts ... I will return.'

Women in the crowd ululated their approval and men stomped and cheered. Mandela's words had been well chosen.

Government was not impressed.

In May 1988, Botha established a four-man committee to handle talks with the rest of the ANC leadership; the members were General Willemse (head of prisons), Niel Barnard, Barnard's assistant Mike Louw and Fanie van der Merwe (a constitutional expert). All four had already been involved in talks with Mandela.

On 18 January 1989, Botha suffered a mild stroke and was attended by his personal physician, Dr Wouter Basson, head of Project Coast and its chemical and biological warfare programme (and dubbed 'Dr Death' in later TRC hearings). On 2 February, Botha resigned as head of the National Party; a Federal Council meeting on 13 March called for his resignation as president. A furious Botha announced elections for 6 September 1989 and then, on 5 July, stunned critics by courteously entertaining Mandela to tea and cake at Tuynhuys, the presidential quarters abutting Parliament. This did not appease those within National Party ranks who feared Botha's erratic conduct was damaging the country; six weeks later Botha was forced to resign by his cabinet.

One of the contenders in the leadership tussle was the conservative De Klerk, who belonged to a sect of the Reformed Church that was so conservative that its members were not allowed to dance. His then wife, Marike, had in previous speeches been quoted as referring to coloured people as 'non-persons' who were South Africa's 'leftovers'. His rival was the long-time Foreign Minister Pik Botha, who was popular in English circles and among liberal Afrikaners.

As the first blossoms of spring fell and coated newly green lawns with pink and cream showers, De Klerk was elected president. Two months later he scrapped the National Security Management System, which organised civilians into officials of the state security system under the SSC. He also downgraded the SSC, making the cabinet the highest policy-making body. The stage was set for one of the most remarkable transitions to democracy the world has yet seen.

The path to power

The regime has its own strategy and part of it will be to ensure that Mandela does not bring on a revolution for them.

Oliver Tambo
At an emergency meeting of the
ANC National Working Committee,
28 October 1988

our LEADERS
Mandela
Kathrada
Mbeki
Mhlaba
nd all POLITICAL PRISONERS

THE BIGGEST DILEMMA facing the National Party government in the 1980s was the realisation that Mandela's release would symbolise the release of every black South African from apartheid, and hasten the end of white minority rule. The ANC was concerned that the government might try to trick ANC activists into revealing themselves, to imprison or kill them. While the ANC believed the struggle could be won only by military means, it lacked the forces, equipment and funds to do this.

The 1985 Kabwe conference, the ANC's first consultative conference in exile since the 1969 Morogoro conference, said it was time 'for us to sue for the expulsion of apartheid South Africa from the UN, to push for practical measures by the international community based on the rejection of the Pretoria regime as illegitimate'. It was perhaps the most important conference of the decade for the ANC. Friends in the United States came to the fore and on 2 October 1986 The Comprehensive Anti-Apartheid Act, sponsored by Representative William Gray of Pennsylvania and propelled by Senators Tom Harkin and Edward Kennedy, became law despite a presidential veto from Ronald Reagan; nothing had a greater impact on hastening the end of apartheid. Other countries rapidly followed and soon South Africa faced concerted universal disapproval, with the punishing effect of political, economic, sports, military and arts sanctions.

But before and after that repression intensified. On 20 July 1985 a partial State of Emergency was declared that soon encompassed the whole country. This continued for four years, becoming ever more repressive. Four months after the State of Emergency was declared, and with thousands of black South Africans imprisoned, the ANC presented their conditions for negotiations to the National Party government – the Harare Declaration – which became the blueprint for change. South African Deputy Minister of Information Louis Nel dismissed the declaration, saying the government had no intention of having talks with the ANC.

But a month later government spokesmen demonstrated a potential shift, when they said government would talk to the ANC and release Mandela if they renounced violence. This condition was rejected by the ANC; in historical hindsight it appears clear that both were preparing for change, but for those living through the dark days of the late 1980s with intense repression, division and death squads it felt as though progress was becoming harder, not easier. The ANC continued to prepare to assume power, and by 1988 had released a set of constitutional guidelines. This approach of policy-making before power made the ANC rare among liberation movements.

Plans to release Mandela were discussed by the State Security Council (SSC), whose ideas ranged from the bizarre to the sinister. The government leaked news that it might release him in return for the freedom of Soviet dissidents Anatoly Shcharansky and Andrei Sakharov, hoping to win American and Soviet approval. It was ignored. SSC ideas included liberating Mandela outside South Africa, into the Transkei (apartheid homeland of the Eastern Cape) or to a villa on Robben Island, or freedom 'in exchange for something else'.

The ANC policy statement of 8 January 1986, delivered by Oliver Tambo, contained a veiled message to Mandela: 'Our strength lies in our unity. We must guard that unity like the apple of our eye.' The ANC called for a grand alliance against apartheid, incorporating businesspeople, whites, Afrikaners and opinion

The struggle is really not about Mandela, it is about other issues.

Joe Slovo
Special Meeting of the National Working Committee of the ANC, Lusaka, 15 October 1989

OPPOSITE: United States civil right leader Jesse Jackson embraces Oliver Tambo during an anti-apartheid demonstration in London in 1985.

PREVIOUS PAGES: A protest march in 1986 demanding the release of imprisoned ANC leaders – Nelson Mandela, Walter Sisulu, Ahmed Kathrada, Govan Mbeki and Raymond Mhlaba – and all other political prisoners.

makers, to force government to the negotiating table by 1990. Their deadline proved astonishingly prescient. By 1987, Mandela had sent clandestine messages to the ANC giving notes on talks with government.

While the ANC declared 1987 the 'Year of the Advance to People's Power', it was sceptical about Mandela's talks. In a highly confidential memo from its National Executive Committee (NEC) meeting (5–9 October 1987), it noted it would consider its position on negotiations, and would brief the ANC membership, the Mass Democratic Movement (MDM) (the successor to the then banned UDF), the frontline states and all socialist countries.

The ANC was aware that there was a different feeling in the air: some business groups were circuitously trying to sound others out about the ANC, while many made direct contact. Tambo said in 1989: 'We have said the regime should create a climate for negotiations by releasing Nelson Mandela. If they do we can say that it does demonstrate, in part, a willingness. The British have said the regime cannot hope to negotiate unless Nelson Mandela is released and the ban on the ANC is lifted. The regime will not hurry to lift the ban ... The armed struggle would have to be stepped up even before Nelson Mandela goes out, so that there is no question of his release being conditional on renouncing armed struggle or that the armed struggle will be abandoned because he is out ... '.

But the ANC was not yet ready for the vision of Mandela, or his belief that only by healing rifts with one's enemies could peace be forged. As a result of the ANC's three decades of exile, paranoia often clouded its judgement.

Not long after this, Tambo became very ill and was sent to London, where his family lived. At a meeting of the ANC's National Working Committee (NWC) on 15 August 1989, Alfred Nzo, then Secretary-General, said: 'The doctors made a categoric statement that ORT [Tambo] has not suffered a stroke. They said a brief spasm in the vein had momentarily denied the brain oxygen and his condition was owing to that. But they said his nervous reactions were not normal. Generally they were satisfied OR's condition was not very serious.' This was not an accurate summation of Tambo's true condition, and he never fully recovered.

Events were proceeding rapidly. PW Botha's autocratic style was seeing increasing resistance from his colleagues. By August, and the NWC meeting, news had filtered through of PW Botha's resignation. This, with news of an election to be held in September in South Africa, led Steve Tshwete, a member of the ANC's National Executive Committee, to '... express the view that the mere announcement that PW Botha has resigned should not impel us to discuss the internal situation'.

Communist Party deputy chief Joe Slovo countered: 'The NWC has devoted 88 percent of its time to discussing negotiation manoeuvres ... a style is creeping in where we allow international events to influence the working of this NWC.' Although the time to govern was nearing, many ANC leaders did not seem to recognise the import of what was happening.

Mandela was covertly keeping the ANC briefed from prison, but not everyone was giving his missives the attention they deserved. With Mandela's old friend Oliver Tambo ill in a Stockholm clinic, a curious inertia began to grip the organisation, and key leaders like Thabo Mbeki were rarely in the Frontline States. The ANC began to be propelled by the MDM within South Africa, even though that organisation, buffered by ongoing arrests and repression, was battling to remain cohesive.

The month after De Klerk was voted into office, the 16 October NEC meeting in Lusaka noted that cleric and MDM leader, the Reverend Allan Boesak '... had called for the regime to

OPPOSITE: Chris Hani, a popular leader of the ANC military wing, Umkhonto we Sizwe, was beloved before he was assassinated by white right-wingers in 1994. He would have almost certainly been a popular contender for president after Mandela.

be given six months and if nothing happened, for an intensification of sanctions'. This call drove the South African government to move faster. A scant four months after Boesak's, call De Klerk agreed to lift restrictions on banned organisations and individuals and to free Mandela.

MK leader Chris Hani was of the opinion that: 'The question of NM's [Mandela's] release ought to be taken out of De Klerk's hands ... there should be a lot of organisation for a march on Victor Verster to demand the unconditional release of NM. The question of achieving results is important and rural organisations such as Inyadza, Contralesa, should be harnessed.'

The ANC was concerned that if De Klerk introduced radical reforms, such as unbanning organisations and releasing Mandela, it would give him credibility and lead to a world prepared to continue to accept white leadership over a black majority populace. But the ANC underestimated international determination for a real transfer of power in South Africa and the wash of optimism and determination that would sweep across South Africa with Mandela's release, making any political solution short of true liberation an exercise in redundancy.

There was another factor implicit in Hani's comments: over the years the ANC had shifted its focus to urban areas, but the ongoing violence in the province of Natal (now KwaZulu-Natal) made it realise the importance of mobilisation in rural areas. As would become apparent during bloody township battles in the 1990s, destabilisation in the rural areas could quickly lead to extensive bloodshed in urban areas. Slovo cautioned: 'We have had in our history a civic guard movement which the regime used for its purposes. Unless we have the capacity to control such organs, they get out of hand.'

His words were prophetic. Some three years later, when violence was gripping East Rand townships and KwaZulu-Natal, the ANC began training and arming township youth into, what it called, self-defence units. While many of these units did protect citizens, most got out of hand and terrorised communities, waging war on opponents or becoming involved in organised criminal activity.

By 1989 repression was so entrenched the ANC was concerned that they would lose the gains of the 1980s as activists became exhausted, their ranks depleted by jailings and police murders. Early in January 1989, Thabo Mbeki reported, after meeting MDM leaders Murphy Morobe and Mohammed Valli Moosa, that: 'The UDF is banned ... the leadership of the UDF is characterised by immobility. Murphy Morobe describes it by saying it is as if they are stunned ... There is a broad leadership in the country which has an ANC orientation, but they act within narrow perimeters.'

And the ANC continued to relegate the opinions of Mandela to a subsidiary level – this was an early indicator of the tensions that prevail to this day between those who led the ANC in exile, and those who supported and occupied leadership positions in the MDM within the country during the darkest days of apartheid. At a special meeting of the NWC on 15 October 1989 in Lusaka, Joe Slovo reported he had seen MDM leader Sydney Mufamadi in London: 'He reported that when the MDM heard the release [of eight Rivonia Trialists including Walter Sisulu] was about to happen and that NM wanted to see a delegation they suspected he wanted to counsel a low key reception. The MDM opposed this.

'NM proceeded to give them a detailed picture of the negotiations that had been going on. He dealt with the history of the releases, how he had negotiated the release of Harry Gwala and Govan Mbeki. He had been critical that they [Gwala and Mbeki] had not been low key and HG's [Gwala's] pictures addressing meetings in an agitated mood had been shown to him. He had not raised his own position, but said the undertaking with the regime was that they play it low key. He said he had seen all seven before their removal [from prison] and they had agreed to play a low key. Sydney said the delegation had come back surprised but they did not hammer the need for the leaders to stand at the head of the mobilisation campaign.

'We discussed this [report] in London – about six of us including Ronnie Kasrils, Aziz Pahad, Gertrude Shope and Thabo Mbeki – in short the feeling was that the correct thing was for them [the released leaders] to take their place at the head of the struggle ... We said they must not be low key.' But, the released leaders ignored this command from London and obeyed Mandela's directive; they did nothing to jeopardise a delicate process.

At the Lusaka report-back, Slovo continued: 'We felt it would be a tragedy if the momentum, the greatest generated in recent history could be deflated. The struggle is really not about Mandela, it is about other issues. He will be released not because of his own recognizances, but because of the ANC.' And this would continue to be the party line from the external members, as we read earlier from Ben Turok, and it was one that was entirely inaccurate; the global

There are four things you have to learn as a prisoner. First, there are the walls. You can see the walls and forever be a prisoner, or you can break through and have the whole world before you in your mind. The second is the warders. Some were very harsh. The third challenge is your friends and comrades. Some people you were very close to outside are impossible to live with in prison. And the fourth, and greatest, challenge is yourself. The enemy within. You have to work with and change yourself.

Tokyo Sexwale
(Former Robben Island prisoner and first premier of Gauteng)

OPPOSITE: Archbishop Desmond Tutu leads a service in Soweto, Johannesburg, in May 1988, marking the end of a two-day convocation attended by church leaders from various denominations to discuss non-violent action against apartheid.

community was gripped first by the suffering of the people of South Africa, second by the dignified approaches of Mandela. Because of those factors the ANC was notable; it was not the other way around.

Mandela never saw himself as more than a disciplined member of a movement of millions, as he made clear in a letter written to PW Botha shortly before he had tea with him at Botha's office in Tuynhuys. They were the same offices that Mandela would occupy less than a decade later. In the 10-page letter, Mandela wrote to Botha: 'I now consider it necessary in the national interest for the ANC and the government to meet urgently to negotiate an effective political settlement.

'At the outset I must point out that I make this move without consultation with the ANC. I must stress that no prisoner, irrespective of his status or influence, can conduct negotiations of this nature from prison ... the question of my release from prison is not an issue, at least at this stage of the discussions ... A government which used violence against blacks many years before we took up arms has no right whatsoever to call on us to lay down arms ... No dedicated ANC member will ever heed a call to break with the SACP. We regard such a demand as a purely divisive government strategy. It is a call on us to commit suicide.

'Two central issues will have to be addressed at such a meeting: firstly, the demand for majority rule in a unitary state; secondly, the concern of white South Africa over this demand, as well as the insistence of whites on structural guarantees that majority rule will not mean domination of the white minority by blacks.'

In 1989 the ANC found events were moving fast. The ANC had planned that '... in the build up to or after the release [of Mandela] there should be systematic effective actions of MK to create the necessary atmosphere for action. These actions should strictly be directed at targets in keeping with movement policy and should be accompanied by propaganda with slogans such as: Welcome home dear commander. None of these operations should be conducted in or close to areas where NM would be at any particular moment.'

However, because De Klerk did not give forewarning of his decision, and because ANC management was so chaotic at that time, these plans came to nought. Political change developed its own momentum.

The unbanning of the ANC and the release of Mandela found the ANC in the eye of a hurricane. The world's media, which had been beating a regular path to its door since 1988, now descended upon Lusaka en masse. MK soldiers, who dreamed they would march down the highways of Pretoria and Johannesburg in military battalions, atop tanks, with crowds cheering and streamers flying, like the images they had seen on old Soviet newsreels, instead returned to a situation none had considered: a negotiated peace and poverty for many. They could find no work. Like Vietnam veterans two decades before who had suffered trauma and psychological anguish at being returned into societies that did not cheer their return, but were embarrassed by their role as combatants, many former soldiers turned to drink, drugs, suicide or crime.

Within hours of his release, on 11 February 1990, Mandela proved himself the greatest of all ANC leaders. At his first press conference, at Bishopscourt, the day after his release, the South African and international press corps, many sceptical whether he would make the grade, gave him a standing ovation. He displayed a warmth and an intellect that impressed all.

Mandela made it clear that he was an obedient cadre of the ANC: 'I intend making only a few preliminary comments at this stage. ... Mr de Klerk ... is a man of integrity who is acutely aware of the dangers of a public figure not honouring his undertakings.' He tried to allay white fears, and condemned the crime that haunted South Africa and terrorised people, regardless of skin colour.

At a Soweto rally on 13 February, he told the enormous crowd sweltering in the heat: 'As proud as I am of the Soweto community I have been greatly disturbed by the statistics of crime I have read in the newspapers. Although I understand the deprivations our people suffer, I must make it clear that the level of crime in our township is unhealthy and must be eliminated as a matter of urgency.'

But when he became president Mandela too did not do enough to fight crime, and by 2011 the police commissioner reported that there were 56,272 people raped in South Africa between March 2010 and April 2011, or 4,689 women, men and children each month. Gender organisations said they believed the real figure was a woman or child raped every 26 seconds. The police commissioner also said that there were 43.6 murders a day in South Africa, a rate six times higher than in the United States, as an example, and greater than in any war zone in the world.

But hope and expectation was high when Mandela spoke to that heaving, sweating, joyful crowd. He continued: 'I stated in 1964 that I, and the ANC, are as opposed to black domination as we are to white domination. We must accept, however, that our statements and declarations alone will not be sufficient to allay the fears of white South Africans. We must clearly demonstrate our goodwill to our white compatriots and convince them by our conduct and argument that a South Africa without apartheid will be a better home for all.'

Mandela re-entered the leadership ranks of the ANC quietly but firmly. At his first meetings with the ANC in Lusaka shortly after his release, he stood with dignity, towering over most of his comrades. He listened more than he spoke at those early meetings, but when he spoke it was with an authority that deterred sceptics

BELOW: A crowd defies armed troops present during a mass funeral, Alexandria, Eastern Cape, during the mid-1980s.

from questioning too strongly. He assumed thoughtful authority in every ANC meeting he would chair. He would not tolerate thoughtlessness, or rhetoric for the sake of cliché-ridden words: he wanted careful thinking, and if he heard considered views he would listen intently, his hands clasped in front of him, and comment only at the end of the discourse. Foolish, shallow thoughts, however, could expect a sharp rebuke. By these means he disciplined his followers to sharpen their focus, improve their information, work harder and strategise more carefully.

The dichotomy between a revolutionary ANC planning to overthrow government and an ANC preparing to govern soon became apparent. As early as 1990 it was noting its concern that there was '... confusion between ANC, Sayco [SA Youth Congress], UDF etc. All go to different areas and do not act in concert. ANC talks of uniting all forces, and chiefs may be present. The next body comes along and says "down with chiefs." We are to blame. We told the youth to make the country ungovernable, but the situation has changed. Our strategy has changed from saying down with everything, to organising the chiefs to be on our side. ... We have not gone to organisations and structures to explain the new strategies. We have to stop conflicting statements and positions.' But again, even in 2011 this was a challenge they had yet to resolve, and that deepened as a global economic crisis dug deeper.

In June 1991 the ANC had its first national conference at home. Hundreds of delegates met at the University of Durban-Westville. They had lunch on the steps of the university, eating *pap* and *vleis* (corn porridge and meat) off polystyrene plates. They exchanged stories of the struggle at home, and of the difficulties of life in exile. Exiles and internal South African activists embraced. Mandela had brought his people home; now they had to settle down to negotiate a democratic future for all.

As the representatives of centuries of white minority rule bowed to the results of the democratic process, the people did, as Martin Luther King Jr did, cry out: Free at last, free at last, thank God Almighty, we are free at last!

Nelson Mandela
Addressing a joint session of the United
States Congress, 6 October 1994

RIGHT: Mandela arrives home in Soweto after his release in 1990. He is flanked (to the right) by his old friend Walter Sisulu and Winnie Madikizela-Mandela.

OPPOSITE: Jubilant Soweto citizens celebrate the release of Mandela at an ANC rally, February 1990.

Crafting a negotiating table

Walk through the door and take your place at the negotiating table together with the government. The time for negotiation has arrived.

President FW de Klerk,
2 February 1990

The question of Nelson Mandela's release ought to be taken out of De Klerk's hands.

Chris Hani
ANC National Executive Committee
meeting minutes, 26 October 1989

DE KLERK DID NOT ASK MANDELA TO GIVE UP VIOLENCE when he released him on 11 February 1990, as PW Botha had when Mandela's release was discussed. But the security and military establishment had little intention of giving up violence; death squads were still operating and detentions continued. It is now clear that De Klerk and some senior politicians did not know this (and had no way of knowing, at least not to the full extent), but, as TRC hearings showed, it was pervasive. As an example, a chemical and biological warfare programme was fully operational despite South Africa signing international treaties in 1974 that it would not develop a chemical warfare enterprise; this programme was adept at assassination and dirty tricks.

In 1990, as an example, the head of Project Coast in the South African National Defence Force, Brigadier Wouter Basson, purchased 500 kilograms of methaqualone, the essential agent for Mandrax (an illicit drug favoured by Cape Flats gangsters and others) from Croatia. Basson's staff told the Truth and Reconciliation Commission in 1998 that it was intended for the manufacture of tear gas. However, TRC commissioners suspected a more sinister motive – they sought to establish whether South Africa's chemical and biological warfare programme was selling drugs to South Africa's black youth. They did not succeed in their quest but as they saw it the thinking was self-evident: if you could not beat them politically, you might as well destroy them with drugs.

Certainly ANC activists found that when they tried to hold meetings or canvass support in the Cape Flats area, close to the beautiful city of Cape Town, they were forced out by drug lords. South Africa remains the world's biggest consumer of illicit methaqualone.

At that time the ANC and National Party tried to use covert means against each other – leaders spoke beautiful words while digging their heels into their opponents' backs. Govan Mbeki said: 'This was a war without absolute winners. African nationalism and Afrikaner nationalism, the two major political forces in South Africa, had fought to a draw ... . Negotiations were the only option left to arrive at a settlement that would encompass all the people of South Africa. And so it happened that the oppressor and the oppressed came together to chart the road to a democratic South Africa.'

De Klerk promised a 'new South Africa, a totally changed South Africa' upon his election in September 1989.

But to do this, he first had gone through a remarkable process of changing himself in the preceding years. De Klerk was a surprising convert to a profound belief in the

PREVIOUS PAGES: Cyril Ramaphosa, Nelson Mandela and Joe Slovo during a 1992 march to commemorate the 1976 Soweto student uprising.

RIGHT: A rally held in Soweto to welcome home the seven ANC leaders, among them Walter Sisulu, Elias Motsoaledi and Wilton Mkwayi, who were released on 15 October 1989.

importance of negotiations and the transfer of power to black rule. There was little to suggest that conservative De Klerk, who had imposed restrictive legislation against universities when he was Minister of Education, had a Damascene conversion.

De Klerk, a devout Christian, belonged to the Dutch Reformed Church that had provided the theological basis to apartheid in the late 1930s.

His branch of the church, the Doppers, were profoundly conservative; they would not allow blacks to enter and took harsh action against those pastors who tried to inspire change. Dominee Pieter Dumans, as an example, was expelled by the church in December 1987, allegedly for breaking the fifth commandment, 'Honour thy father and mother', and the ninth, 'Thou shalt not bear false witness', after he swore in a coloured man as the church's first elder. It is hard, in the 21st century, to see how the church equated his act with those two commandments, but indeed it did. In July 1988, Dumans was reinstated after approaching the Supreme Court, which ruled in his favour. But even on readmission to the church, he was forbidden from administering sacraments or from ministering to his congregation.

De Klerk's office quietly confided in journalists and diplomats, after his election, that the opening of parliament the following year would reveal dramatic reforms. Visas for foreign journalists, usually difficult to obtain, became freely available.

Could De Klerk, newspaper analysts asked, as a devout follower of a church with such strict dictates, have the courage to bring about reforms? It seemed unlikely, but what was certain was that the nation was exhausted by apartheid, sanctions and decades of repression.

Is it politically correct to continue preaching peace and non-violence when dealing with a government whose barbaric practices have brought so much suffering and misery to Africans?

Nelson Mandela
(Secretary of the National Action Council of South Africa), Review of 29, 30, 31 May General Strike, 1961

ABOVE: In Pretoria, members of the fascist Afrikaner Weerstandsbeweging (Afrikaner Resistance Movement) protest against FW de Klerk's reforms and the imminent release of Mandela, February 1990.

Yet on 13 September 1989, the day before his installation as president, De Klerk astounded the country by giving permission for 20,000 anti-apartheid activists to march in Cape Town.

Inspired by this, Thabo Mbeki, Jacob Zuma, Steve Tshwete and those who formed the ANC President's Committee held the first of a series of meetings with the Afrikaner Broederbond, the ideological wing of the National Party, a few weeks later. These were the first real negotiating platforms between the exiled ANC and the Broederbond. On 9 October, Thabo Mbeki told the ANC's National Executive Committee that the Broederbond said that the release of key political prisoners was to begin, and that Mandela would be released last. The minutes of that meeting record Mbeki as saying: 'The *broeders* identified obstacles to change as follows: The NP does not want to lose control of the pace of change; fear of black domination; De Klerk's desire to restructure the state machinery because he does not like the State Security Council; mistrust of the ANC. Regime not happy with the idea that the Harare OAU [Organisation of African Unity] declaration be tabled to the UN which will make it mandatory. It was explained to them that the intervention of the international community will be a matter of negotiation.'

De Klerk wasted no time after being elected president. A month later, on 15 October, he released all Rivonia Trialists except Mandela. On 16 November, he scrapped the Separate Amenities Act, provoking a strong reaction from some right-wing communities. In Bethal, Mpumalanga, the town councillors filled the town swimming pool with soil to prevent black people swimming in it. At Ermelo, some 100 kilometres northeast of Bethal, a man with a *sjambok* (a plastic whip) beat three black children who dared swim in the town's pool with white children. A horrified white mother videotaped the incident and it became an international news story.

The ANC was left off-balance by this rapid change. In a discussion document, *Unbanning of ANC, some strategic considerations*, it noted that it should rapidly try to build its military wing in a way that would not cause De Klerk to backtrack nor the ANC to lose face. It faced the challenge of how to conduct itself as a legal organisation. It began tussling with the issues surrounding the return of exiles and the guarantees it would need for their safety and their resettlement.

BREAKING THROUGH

On the morning of 2 February 1990, offices all around South Africa stopped work as employees crowded around radios and televisions to hear the news most hoped for. And it came. De Klerk said in parliament: 'The time has come to break out of the cycle of violence and break through to peace and reconciliation. The silent majority is yearning for this.' He then scrolled through a litany of organisations the government was unbanning, and a list of repressive legislation it was sweeping aside. He told a hushed parliament that no final date had been set for Mandela's release but he wanted to 'bring the matter to finality without delay'. He endorsed his party's commitment to privatisation – at the time the ANC was committed to nationalisation.

Some South Africans wept. Others sent for Champagne, which they drank in their offices. Still others sat in huddled circles, trying to evaluate what this would mean for their lives. I was in the *Business Day* offices in downtown Johannesburg. Spontaneous applause broke out from journalists who were trained not to show emotion, and then from the street came the sound of a rustling like a deep wind moving through. Outside the window, deep in the gully between buildings, hundreds of people had started walking, silently, with no particular direction, they were now free to move where and how they wanted. Mandela's freedom took a yoke off millions of shoulders.

Share prices soared on the Johannesburg Stock Exchange. A protest march outside parliament evaporated after the news. Anglican Archbishop Desmond Tutu hailed De Klerk. The ANC leadership, which was visiting the ailing Oliver Tambo in his Stockholm clinic, was surly and barely commented – in truth the organisation was bitterly divided as to how it should respond. Leadership was at odds and failing at precisely the time it needed to be present. The Mass Democratic Movement (MDM), the ANC's internal organisation, stepped up to the plate and gave the appropriate response. It said the reforms were 'progressive' and welcomed the 'boldness of some of the steps'. That night, parties were held across the country.

Cyril Ramaphosa, Secretary-General of the National Union of Mineworkers and an MDM leader, was recuperating from pneumonia in a Johannesburg clinic. He had been reading Barbara Tuchman's seminal work, *The March of Folly*, about political folly; he tossed the book to one side and, on a telephone in his private ward, he began urgent consultations with Mohammed Valli Moosa, Sydney Mufamadi, Murphy Morobe and other MDM leaders. A plane was chartered and put on standby for them to fly to Cape Town for Mandela's imminent release. Everyone associated with the ANC was preparing for power, and hoping not to repeat the mistakes of the past.

The time has come to break out of the cycle of violence and break through to peace and reconciliation. The silent majority is yearning for this.

President FW de Klerk,
2 February 1990

What is tragic is that so heroic a figure as Ms Madikizela-Mandela, with her own rich history of contribution to the struggle, became embroiled in a controversy that caused immeasurable damage to her reputation.

Truth and Reconciliation Commission of South Africa Report, Volume Two, October 1998

When he received word from his friends who were negotiating with Mandela that their old leader would be released the next day, Ramaphosa – who many in the years to come would want as a successor to Mandela – pulled the drips from his arms, quickly dressed and caught a chartered plane with them to Cape Town. He would never have time to recuperate adequately from the debilitating effects of pneumonia; in this instance adrenaline was the best antidote.

On 11 February, Mandela walked out of the gates of Victor Verster Prison in Paarl, hand-in-hand with his wife Winnie. That evening he read a carefully crafted, dull speech, honed and argued over by ANC and MDM leaders, from Cape Town's Grand Parade. United States civil

LEFT: Mandela walks to freedom from Victor Verster prison on 11 Februrary 1990 with his wife Winnie.

rights leader Jesse Jackson ripped his suit climbing a fence in an unsuccessful attempt to be near Mandela. Ramaphosa, with a plaster marking the spot where the drip had been removed from his hand, held Mandela's microphone and put himself between him and an enthusiastic crowd.

The National Reception Committee wanted Mandela to go home to Soweto that night, but events in Cape Town were more chaotic than any could have anticipated (among other things, the driver bringing Mandela from the prison to Cape Town got lost and Mandela had to ask a startled suburban couple for directions). Archbishop Tutu was at Cape Town City Hall when organisers told him Mandela would stay at his home in elite Bishopscourt that night. 'Mandela

ABOVE: Walter Sisulu, Nelson Mandela and Cyril Ramaphosa during Mandela's first public address in 27 years, at Cape Town's Grand Parade, 11 February 1990.

During my lifetime I have dedicated myself to this struggle of the African people. I have fought against white domination, and I have fought against black domination. I have cherished the ideal of a democratic and free society in which all persons live together in harmony and with equal opportunities. It is an ideal which I hope to live for and achieve. But if needs be, it is an ideal for which I am prepared to die.

Nelson Mandela
During his trial in 1963

was concerned that if he was staying in Cape Town it should not be in a white area, but his security detail were concerned that they would not be able to control a township situation. Trevor Manuel [who years later would become Finance Minister] and Dullah Omar [Mandela's Cape Town lawyer] convinced Mandela that I had transformed Bishopscourt into a people's place. When he arrived he immediately went into a meeting. Walter Sisulu and most of the leadership were there, but what we did do once they had all gathered was to pray. We said the Lord's Prayer and sang a Xhosa hymn, 'Masibulele Kayesu' (let us say thank you Jesus). But he kept getting calls, we'd answer the phone and people would say, "This is the White House", "This is President Kaunda". My wife Leah was in Soweto, but I was helped by staff and friends. We coped. My physician, Ingrid le Roux, is a Swedish doctor, and she was the first doctor to see him in freedom, something she cherishes very much.'

I was called by members of the NRC to find temporary accommodation for his first night in Johannesburg, and I did. It was the simple but expansive and secluded home of a friend in Honeydew, close to where Northgate Mall now is. She was the single mother of five children and removed her excited brood from the house for one night while Mandela stayed there with Winnie before his return to Soweto.

STEEP CLIMB

Mandela's long walk to freedom had ended; now the steep climb to democracy began. Reflecting on those difficult early days, Mac Maharaj said, 'The great men and women who stand out in history have all been driven by the need to remove suffering and injustice. What is startling about them is that, although most of them have suffered, they transcend bitterness about their own personal misfortunes. They are moved by the suffering of others. Their suffering is submerged in their quest for a better world. The only time we glimpse inside Nelson Mandela is when he reflects on his own family. Then you see his pain and the anguish … But betray him or his cause, and Madiba turns to icy steel.'

'De Klerk learnt this lesson the hard way when he failed to stop the violence in the early 1990s. From being described by Madiba on his release as "a man of integrity", De Klerk later withered in every public encounter with Mandela. … Just as democracy could not have been achieved without an organised political force, so too is the realisation of transformation of our country impossible without the ANC leading the process. The struggle to bring about such fundamental changes has always been accompanied by another very different struggle – that of making the ANC the effective instrument it needs to be. There are many lessons from our past with great relevance for the challenges we face.'

Confronting the endemic violence in South Africa horrified returning ANC members. It was one thing discussing violence and watching it on foreign news, but the intensity of violence in

KwaZulu-Natal and the townships flanking Johannesburg shocked them. The cordial backslapping of the Groote Schuur Minute, when key members of the ANC's National Executive Committee met with government, was soon replaced by horror.

The Groote Schuur Minute of May 1990 established a working group to make recommendations on the definition of a political offence, as well as devising the mechanisms for the release of political prisoners and granting of immunity. In a clumsily worded note, laden with bureaucratic terms, it noted: 'Temporary immunity from prosecution for political offences committed before today will be considered on an urgent basis for members of the National Executive Committee and selected other members of the ANC from outside the country to enable them to return and help with the establishment and management of political activities to assist in bringing violence to an end.'

The ANC delegation, consisting of seven black and two white people and one mixed race (or coloured) and one Indian person (nine men and two women), was selected to make a statement about racial equality and gender sensitivity. The government delegation was nine men, all white, all Afrikaner. The ANC demanded 20,000 to 40,000 exiles be allowed to return home. In the minutes of the ANC National Working Committee of 11 May 1990, the belief was recorded that the 'De Klerk delegation appeared determined to achieve progress. De Klerk cautioned about romanticising the armed struggle, it was rhetoric he observed that encouraged "street violence".'

The ANC operated out of offices loaned to it by Munich Re insurance company opposite the offices of *The Star* newspaper in downtown Johannesburg. Sympathisers loaned computers, fax machines, cars and their services. At the time I was an opinion editorial and analysis writer for the *Los Angeles Times* and that newspaper had a forerunner to Google that captured the world's

BELOW: The ANC delegation to the Groote Schuur Minute of May 1990: (front row from left) Ruth Mompati, Alfred Nzo, Nelson Mandela, Joe Slovo, Walter Sisulu and Cheryl Carolus; (back row from left) Archie Gumede, Ahmed Kathrada, Joe Modise, Beyers Naudé and Thabo Mbeki.

news and ran it as an ongoing stream. I loaned a computer to the office with this necessary resource for the publicity department. My action echoed those of very many others who helped in whatever way they could; we all hoped for a peaceful, socially just outcome for South Africa.

In late July, police uncovered Operation Vula (the opening) which had been set up in 1988 as a network of ultra-secret MK cells. De Klerk was furious, and the securocrats in his establishment tried to persuade him to cut off talks. But he was angry, not stupid: he had begun a process that had to continue.

The next round of top-level talks took place the following month. The Pretoria Minute was signed at the Presidency in Pretoria on 6 August 1990. The final report, dated 21 May 1990, of the working group on political offences, was accepted. The meeting instructed the working group to draw up a plan for the release of ANC prisoners and the granting of indemnity in a phased manner and to report before the end of August. The further release of prisoners was set to begin on 1 September 1990. Indemnities would begin from 1 October 1990, and be complete before the end of the year, to enable the return of exiles. These were all wishful deadlines. Talks embraced a labyrinth of operational details, bureaucracies to be waded through, and humane considerations, such as pre-release counselling for prisoners and housing exiles, that made those first deadlines impossible to fulfil.

The most important, and controversial, announcement, was that the ANC would 'suspend all armed actions with immediate effect. No further armed actions and related activities by the ANC and its military wing Umkhonto we Sizwe will take place.' Both delegations expressed serious concern about the high levels of violence and intimidation in the country, especially in the then province of Natal. They agreed that it was vital that understanding should grow among all sections of the South African population '... problems can and should be solved through negotiations'. Both parties committed themselves to undertake measures '... to promote and expedite the normalisation and stabilisation of the situation in line with the spirit of mutual trust obtaining among the leaders involved'.

Government undertook to lift the State of Emergency in Natal and to begin repealing security legislation. The Pretoria Minute concluded on an upbeat note, that was not to last: 'We are convinced that what we have

Both delegations [of the ANC and government] agreed that it was vital that understanding should grow among all sections of the South African population, that problems can and should be solved through negotiations.

The Pretoria Minute, signed by the National Party government and the ANC, Pretoria, 6 August 1990

agreed upon today can become a milestone on the road to true peace and prosperity for our country. All of us can henceforth walk that road in consultation and cooperation with each other. We call upon all those who have not yet committed themselves to peaceful negotiations to do so now. The way is now open to proceed toward negotiations on a new constitution.'

The next month, however, Mandela made a trip through some African countries, to Europe, Canada and the United States to thank those internationally who had done so much to help end apartheid. In his first day in New York he was honoured with a rare ticker tape parade, and it was estimated that around 75,000 people left their offices and homes to greet him.

But he returned to a country that was in agony. Violence was spiralling out of control. Armed groups attacked people on trains, spraying them with automatic gunfire and throwing them onto railway tracks. Years later at TRC hearings it would be revealed that these were often government death squads. De Klerk denied knowledge of these events at TRC hearings, but enough overall

BELOW: The huge East Rand squatter camp of Phola Park was formed after people fled violence in nearby Zonke'sizwe and were joined by displaced people from other areas. In 1990 incendiary bombs were used to burn down part of the squatter camp. Residents accused police of complicity with Inkatha in this attack.

ABOVE: 'Usuthu, usuthu.' This deep
chant from approaching Zulu impis
terrified every township resident in
Gauteng in the early 1990s, as terrible
clashes daily claimed the lives of
dozens. This impi from Vosloorus on
the East Rand prepares for battle.

evidence came out to suggest that, although he might not have known about every incident of the hundreds, or even thousands, that occurred, he certainly knew of some.

Mandela, faced with media coverage of people being hacked with pangas, and of police massacres, was incensed. The minutes of the ANC National Executive Committee of 12 and 13 September 1990 show that, seven months after government had unbanned the ANC and long before either the return of exiles or major releases of political prisoners, the ANC wanted to suspend negotiations.

The minutes read: 'Reports on the violence indicate the deep involvement of the police with Inkatha. Residents reported that in Phola Park incendiary bombs were used to burn down the squatter camp. Police wearing balaclavas had accompanied those wearing red bands. Threats were made against those sheltering refugees ... People accused the ANC of doing nothing to protect them. People were publicly tearing up their membership cards. There was the fear that unless we took the initiative, police would begin arming both sides leading to an escalation in conflict. It was said the people would defend themselves but in a way that is ill disciplined, revenge seeking and not as effective unless we deploy trained people to assist and establish a framework within which such self-defence should take place. This must not be done in secret.'

There was an appeal for a central body of self-defence units. The minutes noted 'extensive discussion was held on the recommendation by the deputy president [Mandela] that we suspend the talks. It was agreed that an extraordinarily extended National Executive Committee meeting be called to consider the suspension of talks with the regime. The time has come for us to tell De Klerk that he settles the issue of violence within seven days or talks are suspended.'

A few days later, on 18 September 1990, Mandela called an emergency extended session of the National Executive Committee where he detailed a bitter meeting between him and De Klerk. Mandela questioned police involvement in killings. He told the National Executive Committee De Klerk had denied this. Mandela reported him as saying '... the security forces were behind them on peace initiatives.' Mandela pointed out to De Klerk that there had been 4,000 deaths in Natal and 700 in the townships flanking Johannesburg, with pitifully few arrests and no signs of violence abating. De Klerk responded: 'There is a third force orchestrating the violence and government has taken the decision to weed out those elements.' General Constand Viljoen, who was head of the army, chipped in, 'There is no third force in the sense of an independent organisation but there are mischievous elements.'

Mandela challenged the readiness with which the security forces opened fire on township residents. He opposed government's intended erection of razor wire around hostels inhabited by rural workers to the cities and towns, even though publicly the ANC was calling for this. He pointed out that some hostels were already fenced, '... but police have allowed armed troublemakers to come out'.

Mandela said that he, Penuell Maduna, Zola Skweyiya and Mathews Phosa had met with police commissioner General Johan Coetzee, General van Heerden and Tim McNally, the attorney general of Natal, to push for arrests and convictions. But to little avail. The National Executive Committee meeting became heated as ANC Natal leader Harry Gwala launched into a spluttering diatribe: 'People in Natal are now living in the bush, they are being hunted down. The choice is either they join Inkatha or face death. The police are visiting locations and telling people they have no need of arms since ANC has stopped armed struggle. People are calling on the ANC to enable them to defend themselves.' Mandela replied, 'What response can we give to that request?' None had an answer. Mandela mused, 'What we need is pressure to stop government duplicity.'

Anger within the tripartite alliance of the ANC, the Congress of South African Trade Unions (Cosatu) and the South African Communist Party (SACP) was intense. All had family or friends who had to flee their homes, or who had been killed or injured. At a later tripartite alliance meeting the decision taken on 6 August to suspend the armed struggle was attacked. Mandela found his motives questioned. A comment at the meeting summed it up: 'We operate as though it is possible to enter into gentleman's agreements with the regime.' Some pressed for international mediation, while others said: 'We must stipulate deadlines linked to mass action.'

Mandela began responding in stronger language – the situation was deteriorating in a way that saw his credibility and leadership on the line. On 11 December he wrote to the heads of government attending the European Community Summit to request that decisions on sanctions be postponed until early 1991.

'Despite all our efforts we have as yet not succeeded in removing the obstacles to negotiations as visualised in the UN General Assembly Declaration on South Africa adopted last December. The overwhelming majority of political prisoners have as yet not been released and people continue to be detained without trial, to mention only two obstacles. The important agreement we reached with the government on the 6th of August to begin exploratory talks on constitutional matters has not yet been implemented, owing to the refusal of the government to begin these talks.' Now the mettle and leadership of Mandela would be tried as never before.

A clash of values

Walk through the door and take your place at the negotiating table together with the government. The time for negotiation has arrived.

Nelson Mandela
Speech in Durban, 25 February 1990

BEFORE HE LEFT PRISON, Mandela wrote to his old friend Mangosuthu Buthelezi, the leader of the Zulu-based Inkatha Freedom Party (IFP), appealing for his help in ending the civil war in Natal. More than 15,000 people had died in conflict that had raged for five years by the time of Mandela's release in 1990. Well over a million had been made refugees in the land of their birth.

Mandela and Buthelezi were introduced by Walter Sisulu in the 1950s. For many years, with the ANC banned and in exile and some of its leaders in jail, Buthelezi carried on many ANC traditions. In 1975, Buthelezi, encouraged by the ANC, launched Inkatha, a Zulu cultural organisation that quickly developed a political face. Inkatha even adopted the ANC's black, green and gold colours. By 1979, opinion polls showed he was more popular than Mandela among black people. However, tensions developed between him and the ANC because of his involvement in the apartheid policy of Bantustans (black homelands to which government gave quasi-independence as a way of trying to keep black people out of 'white' cities – but the terrible poverty and often infertile land in these homelands doomed this policy). Soon, Buthelezi and the ANC openly loathed each other, but violent conflict only emerged in the late 1980s.

Mandela and Buthelezi finally, publicly, met almost a year after Mandela's release. In the interim Mandela appealed to the youth ('the shock troops of the struggle', as he called them) to show understanding toward homeland leaders like Buthelezi. Addressing the South African Youth Congress on 13 April 1990 at KaNyamazane in KaNgwane, Mandela urged: 'I want to appeal to you, not to be unnecessarily hostile against the homeland leaders. These men are our flesh and blood and we want them to join the struggle. We know some went into this system honestly thinking it was an effective option. But those who have discovered their mistakes and are prepared to come to the liberation movement let us welcome them with open arms. There is no need to say because a man has made a mistake before, we should no longer work with him.'

Buthelezi had hoped for a meeting with the ANC since 1989. The ANC's National Working Committee in Lusaka on 7 August 1989, attended by Alfred Nzo, Joe Slovo, Jacob Zuma and others, heard that Buthelezi was demanding, 'For the summit to take place … President Oliver Tambo should personally invite him … . Meeting agreed we ought to keep a record of correspondence with GB [Buthelezi] to expose [at appropriate time] that GB is intent on torpedoing peace talks.'

Old rivalries die hard. An ANC document circulated to senior officials in April 1991, with the unwieldy title *Counter Revolution in the Making – Toward a common perception of violence in the transitional period*, probably hit the nail on the head when it said: 'Violence in any situation is not an end in itself. It pursues given political objectives.' It suggested that government strategy was to 'present itself as a force indispensable to the process of transition both as the manager of the process and the force best placed to secure it'.

But violence spiralled, and no-one could control it. The huge East Rand squatter camp of Phola Park, as an example, which by 1992 had some 45,000 inhabitants, was formed after people fled hostility in nearby Zonke'sizwe. They were joined by displaced people from other areas. In the rutted tracks of the hastily built shantytown, children played mock battles with cardboard shields, sticks for spears and crudely made AK-47s. Early in the same year 10,000 people fled violence from Folweni near Amanzimtoti; and the same happened at Umlazi (4,000) and at Murchison (1,000).

Entire villages were bereft of inhabitants: doors swinging eerily open, chickens pecking in the dirt, goats and pigs searching for food. In graveyards, mounds of red soil always seemed to be

piled next to more freshly dug graves for victims of the latest massacre. The final TRC report blamed the IFP for 4,000 murders, the ANC for 1,000 and the South African Police and KwaZulu police for falling into the next largest category of those responsible for killings in the region. Buthelezi mourned Mandela's failure to approach him directly to negotiate peace. He recalled Mandela's letter written to him from prison: 'Mandela was expressing his anguish and said we should get together because the violence was a shame to us as African leaders. A few days after his release he phoned me to say thank you for his release and wanted me to accompany him to the king [Goodwill Zwelithini] about the violence. I fixed dates for a meeting but it never materialised. It was only much later that he told me radicals like Harry Gwala and others were saying under no circumstances must he meet with me.

'It is a pity, the history of the country would have been quite different. Jointly we may have defused the violence sooner and that would have had its own rewards for us. Later, [when] we went to the Security Council in New York, he described me as a surrogate of the NP. I'd always

ABOVE: Mandela attends a rally in KwaZulu-Natal with ANC leaders from the area, among them Jeff Radebe and Jacob Zuma, both dressed in full Zulu regalia.

PREVIOUS PAGES: An Inkatha Freedom Party official from Dube hostel in Soweto leads an impi on a protest march, 16 March 1996.

Violence in KwaZulu-Natal kept threatening to torpedo transitional negotiations, constitutional talks and the democratic process itself.

placed him on a pedestal when United Democratic Front people and those in exile attacked me. I'd always put him in a class of his own. I was devastated.'

While politicians are able to cause conflict with words, violence, once begun, develops a life of its own and can be manipulated by other forces, political groupings or criminal elements, to their advantage. The murders in townships and rural areas saw relations tense between Mandela and De Klerk after a clash between a Zulu impi (a group of Zulu warriors) and ANC mourners

in July 1990. De Klerk, despite a warning from Mandela that an attack was expected by Inkatha, did nothing to prevent it. In hindsight, Mandela should have probably done more too. The two sides clashed at a funeral in Sebokeng and 32 people died.

Visibly angry, Mandela later told a press conference, 'I said, "You were warned beforehand. You did nothing. Why? Why have there been no arrests? In any other country where 32 people had been slaughtered in this way, the head of state would come out condemning the matter and consoling the next of kin. Why have you not done so?"' De Klerk had no answer.

Instead, on 31 August, government enacted changes to the Zulu code in KwaZulu-Natal (the homeland run by Buthelezi within Natal), that was signed by De Klerk: 'No black shall carry an assegai, wood stick, battle axe, stick shod with iron, staff or sharp-pointed stick or any other dangerous weapon [except] if a person could prove he had the bona fide intention to carry such dangerous weapons in accordance with traditional Zulu usage, customs or religions'.

No other ethnic grouping in the country was accorded similar 'cultural' rights. And so for the first time, in the midst of the killing fields of KwaZulu-Natal, these brutal killing implements attained legitimacy.

The ANC spun into a crisis. The minutes of the ANC National Executive Committee special meeting of 12 and 13 September 1990, chaired by Mandela, noted: 'Reports on the violence indicate the deep involvement of the police with Inkatha.'

There was an appeal for a centrally organised body of self-defence units. These were established but became forces beyond the control of any political leadership.

We had to institute transformation in terms of policies, laws and institutions: budgets, civil service and delivery mechanisms all constitute governance. How do you deliver in an innovative and creative way and transform orthodoxy to revolutionary?

Jay Naidoo
(Former Minister of Posts, Telecommunications and Broadcasting)

The National Executive Committee noted: 'Buthelezi will not simply be satisfied with a meeting with Mandela. He is working with the government and certain international forces. A meeting that ends in failure will be disastrous and violence will become even worse ... . We have made an error in our approach [to government] giving the impression we will not allow anything to stop the negotiating process.'

Mandela was at his wits' end. As part of his efforts to unify a country that had been divided since its birth, he had tried to gain public sympathy for homeland leaders like Buthelezi in open pronouncements. He had incurred criticism from ANC members by repeatedly calling De Klerk a man of integrity and Buthelezi his brother. Not long after his release, he had even suggested to the ANC leadership that Buthelezi, De Klerk and he should visit strife-torn areas together, 'to find out what is happening'. The ANC agreed, but neither De Klerk nor Buthelezi did. The ANC threatened to suspend negotiations on 4 April 1991 after an National Executive Committee meeting, where it demanded that De Klerk comply with a list of seven measures to end violence by 9 May.

Only months before this, the IFP and ANC had held warm, thoughtful, but regrettably often secret, meetings. On 26 September 1990, ANC and IFP officials met and reaffirmed the need to 'end the violence immediately'. Within three weeks, they met again. Journalists, sitting outside the briefing room on 15 October 1990, said the meeting seemed relaxed and friendly, and occasional laughter could be heard. However, no press statement was made other than to say talks had been cordial.

Behind closed doors, the delegation, consisting of John Nkadimeng, Jacob Zuma, Thabo Mbeki, Joe Nhlanhla, Josiah Jele and Joel Netshitenzhe from the ANC, and Frank Mdlalose, ESE Sithebe, VB Ndlovu, ET Bhengu, M Zondi and N Nkehli from the IFP, agreed to a meeting between their leaders. It was a shame that they did not feel the need to take the public into their confidence, because the difficulties, recorded in the minutes, give a deeper understanding of the problems – and also show how trivial some of the issues were that caused war.

BELOW: A displaced woman returns to her home in Sonkombo, KwaZulu-Natal, ahead of the country's first democratic elections in 1994.

The minutes note: 'The main problem within the IFP is that township councillors had not involved other local leaders, particularly the chiefs. These leaders felt left out ... [and] for some people, violence has become a source of revenue; others have emerged as heroes in the violence and it is difficult to sell peace to them.' A further obstacle to peace was, 'Local leaders [from the ANC and IFP] fear being seen in each other's company because this might infuriate their followers. We need local people to get used to solving problems together. This will help resolve problems of unfounded rumours, serve as an example to the people and facilitate the whole process.'

In words that would be echoed over and over again during the next four years, this positive meeting observed, 'Statements from the top can jeopardise local peace initiatives. If one of the

ABOVE: The body of an old man who was slain outside his home in Bambayi township, KwaZulu-Natal, in March 1994.

leaders makes a hostile statement, the grassroots are bound to identify with the statement and it bedevils the whole process. We appeal to leaders at the highest level to assist the committee by not making statements which could undermine the [peace] process.'

There were a number of very secret meetings between Buthelezi and Mandela too, before their first public meeting on 29 January 1991 in Durban. Despite the public smiles and handshakes, at the January meeting it was clear to the huge press corps gathered outside that there were serious tensions. Behind closed doors, Mandela told Buthelezi that the '... violence now escalating in the country is an indictment to the black leadership as a whole. This is not the time to apportion blame. We must accept collective responsibility for what is going on. There is an element of faction fighting in what is going on and it is necessary to recognise there is a third force at work.' Buthelezi accepted the existence of such a third force but said it would require deeper discussion at IFP central committee level.

There were also light moments between the ANC and IFP. Suzanne Vos, an IFP parliamentarian, remembered: 'I flew down for a meeting in Durban. There was a picture of me with the wealthy Sandton branch of the IFP in the newspaper, and Mandela said, "I saw your picture in the paper this morning." Then he said, "Do your members take their cultural weapons to the meetings?" I said, "No, my members just rattle their jewels."'

Sadly, these moments of lightness were rare, and a lot more blood was to flow. In July 1991, secret papers were unearthed by newspapers that showed that the IFP was being funded by government. They also showed that some IFP cadres were being trained in secret military camps by the South African military and were also receiving weapons from them.

Worse was to come. On 17 June 1992, a Zulu impi from KwaMadala hostel, flanking Iscor's steel works, crept across darkened fields to the ANC-supporting settlement of Boipatong and massacred 46 people. A baby had part of his scalp axed off as his mother held him protectively in her arms. Residents claimed at the time, and in testimony to the Goldstone Commission, that police had protected the impi.

Mandela angrily called off talks with government. 'I can no longer explain to our people why we continue to talk to a government that is murdering our people,' he said. De Klerk went to the area, but was forced to flee by furious township residents who beat on his car shouting, 'Go away you dog.' As his car sped off, police opened fire, killing three more residents.

The Goldstone Commission investigations into violence were headed by Judge Richard Goldstone (who, as a testament to his integrity, would become the first chief prosecutor of the United Nations International Criminal Tribunal for the former Yugoslavia and Rwanda, but in 1993 he was tussling with death squads and violence in South Africa). He reported then: 'No-one other than the Inkatha Freedom Party and the ANC have the power to curb the violence and intimidation being perpetrated by their respective supporters ... . Even if allegations against members of the security forces prove to be justified, such misconduct would not have been possible but for the ongoing battle between the ANC and the IFP.'

The commission criticised ANC and IFP leadership for being 'overhasty' in levelling accusations at each other, and for being 'tardy' in taking steps to 'stop the violence by imposing discipline and accountability among membership.'

Prolonged political violence saw the police become paramilitary in nature, and, assisted by security legislation which permitted detention and obliquely condoned torture, the police failed to investigate crime. Criminal statistics became submerged as part of 'the violence'. Ordinary communities began arming themselves and adopting vigilantism to protect themselves, not only against political opponents, but also against the gangs of criminals that roamed free under the mantle of 'the violence'.

BELOW: Hostility between supporters of the IFP and the ANC continued to cause violence in KwaZulu-Natal after the 1994 general election.

ABOVE: Children in Phola Park, near
Thokoza, became involved in
pre-election violence in 1994, with
devastating long-term effects on them
and the communities they lived in.

Some youth who attained political leadership but, because of years of lost schooling, could never obtain jobs, resorted to terror and crime under the guise of political activism.

Courts failed to operate properly, and criminal activity, thus obscured, thrived. This would create the deepest wounds within the future democratic state. Faction fighting, a centuries-old scourge that saw African clans pit themselves against each other, often for decades-old grievances, was allowed to flourish and develop new forms under the haze of violence.

In a series of train massacres, people were thrown out of trains or were shot in their seats as they travelled to work. In one instance an entire carriage of devout Christians, who held church services as they travelled to and from work, were executed as they prayed and sang hymns. TRC hearings heard confessions from the government agents who carried out these atrocities.

The ANC's document on counter-revolution had correctly surmised that, '... the character of the violence engulfing the PWV [now Gauteng] in particular ... is organised counter-revolution carried out by well-trained, professional bandits. The actions are thoroughly planned and while the immediate actors might not have any political programme the controllers are pursuing definite political objectives.

'The actions are characterised by deliberate terrorism. The actions of these units is not an aberration, but reflects the confidence of forces acting within the ambit of state policy with the support of command structures all the way up – the state is creating an excuse for repressive measures – switching violence on or off at given moments to create the impression that the state is indispensable to the achievement of peace in the townships.'

Years later, Buthelezi, who became Home Affairs Minister in Mandela's government, wore the wounds which ANC insults inflicted upon him like medals. Sitting in his parliamentary office in 1998, he said: 'These things are still there, they are not behind us. You can't leave things like that without passing through a period of reconciliation. People cannot say the IFP and ANC can merge. We need to quietly sit and clear this up.'

Buthelezi, who is a decade younger than Mandela, says Mandela was his hero, with the emphasis on *was*. Insiders say Mandela has often come close to bullying in negotiations with Buthelezi, '... which just makes Mangosuthu stubborn'.

As the date set for the election approached, relations worsened between the ANC and Inkatha. Buthelezi began threatening that KwaZulu-Natal would ignore any negotiated settlement (Inkatha had already walked out of talks) and would go it alone. He called for an international negotiated settlement, to which Mandela finally agreed. Ultimately, though, this was a futile publicity ploy.

Elections happened relatively peacefully in KwaZulu-Natal, despite the posturing of politicians. Inkatha amicably settled into the Government of National Unity, with Buthelezi proudly remarking in June 1998, 'So far I have served as acting president nine times when Mandela and Mbeki have been out of the country. It is a world record, and I am not even an ANC member.' On 27 August 1998, a month after Mandela turned 80, Buthelezi celebrated his 70th birthday. He was asked then if he had any intention of retiring. 'No, the work is hard, but it is there to be done.' Was he grooming any successors? 'Having been born an *nkosi* [chief], I would like to enjoy the last years of my life, but I have been born into a tradition of service. I think I have served as best I can. If there were younger leaders who could take over, maybe. But I have always said that when we attained political liberation, that is when the liberation struggle will really begin, and that is only starting now.'

In 2012, as this book went to print, he was still leading his party at the noble age of 83. Calls for him to retire have increased, but as his party's popularity has dwindled he has shown scant interest in relinquishing leadership.

Mandela doesn't walk on water, he roller blades. He has a core of autocratic, ruthless steel.

Senior Inkatha Freedom Party parliamentarian

Transformation

Does it firmly put us on the road to majority
rule and how long will it take?

Nelson Mandela
Discussing a proposed agreement
from the Multiparty Talks, 1993

'LATE ONE NIGHT IN 1993, when we thought that we had finally made a breakthrough after marathon talks, the ANC's negotiation team went to report to Madiba at his Johannesburg home. The president of the ANC had only two questions for his exhausted negotiators: Does it put us firmly on the road to majority rule and how long will it take?' Mac Maharaj pauses and smiles: 'Satisfied with our answers, he gave the interim constitution his blessing.'

Democratic negotiations took place in a huge warehouse surrounded by gum trees and a caravan retailer. Situated close to Johannesburg (now OR Tambo) International Airport, it was the perfect negotiations venue; it had dozens of small offices and rooms for political parties, journalists and other organisations to caucus and hold discussions. The large central hall was big enough to hold the 28 political organisations involved in the multiparty talks, and versatile enough to be split into smaller sections. Talks frequently went on until 2 a.m. or 3 a.m. and resumed not long after dawn had raised a weary head above the horizon. The workers in the canteen adjacent to the hall became accustomed to multiple shifts, and often 18- or 20-hour days; they kept delegates supplied with steaming mugs of coffee or tea, plates of porridge or scrambled eggs for breakfast, and stews for meals later in the day or in the early hours of the morning.

From the start right-wing Afrikaners, joined by foreign hangers-on and some English members, were opposed to the unbanning of organisations and the release of political prisoners. They opposed any

ABOVE: Mandela welcomes his old friend Oliver Tambo back from exile, in December 1990.

PREVIOUS PAGES: President Mandela enters parliament with speaker Frene Ginwala in 1997. Directly behind him is Defence Minister Mosioua 'Terror' Lekota, who is followed by parliamentary secretary Sindiso Mfenyana.

action that recognised the human rights of black people and that could pave the way to majority rule in South Africa.

Between April and mid-July 1990, two people were killed and 48 others injured around Johannesburg in a dozen right-wing bombings directed at places frequented by black people, such as minibus taxi ranks. Arms and ammunition were stolen from police stations, armouries and defence force caches. Some said the leader of the right-wing Afrikaner Weerstandsbeweging, Eugène Terre'Blanche, was an agent for military intelligence and that the bombs were a ploy to destabilise or prevent democratic elections. By the time the TRC hearings had ended in 1998 this accusation did not seem far-fetched but never received the stamp of authenticity. (Years later Terre'Blanche was murdered by farmworkers on his small farm near Ventersdorp.)

David Ottaway, in his book *Chained Together*, wrote that the personal relationship between Mandela and De Klerk '... fell victim to the violence. They became increasingly disillusioned with each other, questioning the ability of the other to deliver his constituency and discovering they held strikingly different views of how the new South Africa should be governed.

Each accused the other of 'talking peace while making war'. The peace process was made more difficult by the failure of both leaders to respect either the letter or the spirit of the first accords they reached. Their challenges were not just with their personal relationship, it extended to those on their side. They spent as much time negotiating with their allies as they did with each other.

Small wonder then, that not a single accord struck between May 1990 and September 1992, whether over the release of political prisoners, the return of exiles, the ANC's hidden arms caches, or the curbing of violence, was carried out on time or according to the letter.

'Mandela launched vicious personal verbal attacks against De Klerk that left one wondering why he was still talking to the state president at all. He also sometimes lacked political courage, shrinking from chastising his own followers for the same excesses in violence he accused ANC opponents of indulging in. ... De Klerk who had the power of the state and its security apparatus to make things happen if he willed, failed to act. It took a third party, Judge Richard Goldstone [who, as has been mentioned earlier in this book, headed a commission investigating state security's role in the political violence], to point out that both Mandela and De Klerk were partly responsible for the political violence, and that both had duties to uphold as the country's two leading statesmen.'

As early as the annual ANC statement on 8 January – this time, the 1991 *Year of Mass Action for Transfer of Power to the People* – Mandela gave the National Executive Committee the view that 'the government will have to take full responsibility for any delay to the constitutional negotiations caused by its failure to implement the agreements entered into at Groote Schuur and Pretoria. We will continue to use all means at our disposal to ensure that these agreements are adhered to, because of their intrinsic importance and their relevance to ... an early start to the process of negotiating a new constitution.'

The ANC wanted the election of a Constituent Assembly to run the negotiations process and establish 'an interim government to oversee the process of transition until a new parliament was elected and a democratic government formed on the basis of the new constitution'. While calling for the police and defence force to end conflict and the South African government to resign, the ANC also 'reaffirmed the right of the people to self-defence. By decision of our Consultative

ABOVE: Strain showing between Mandela and De Klerk at the signing of the National Peace Accord in 1991.

Conference, our movement is committed to assist the people throughout the country to set up the necessary mechanisms for the defence of each community, which mechanisms must enjoy the support and confidence of the people as a whole'.

Mandela read this statement out ponderously in a small office used as the ANC boardroom in a building owned by reinsurers Munich Re, in downtown Johannesburg. Oliver Tambo sat stiffly beside him. This was one of Tambo's first public appearances in South Africa. His son Dali stood at his side, elegant in a black Nehru suit. Journalists sat on the floor, squashed into every available space and spilling out into the passage.

The statement declared, 'We reaffirm our unwavering opposition to any of our members and supporters using force where political discussion is called for, or as a means of promoting any of our campaigns.' The two voices of the ANC were developing a public profile – the one spoke peace, while the other threatened war, but regrettably belligerence did more to fan flames in black areas and lead to unnecessary death. The ANC also said it would liaise with all relevant organisations to 'preclude violent confrontation ... we trust that all these organisations including IFP [Buthelezi's Inkatha Freedom Party] will co-operate with us in genuine good faith to save the lives and property of the people'.

On 29 January 1991, Mandela and Buthelezi discussed ways to find peace in KwaZulu-Natal, but the accord they reached had no meaning among warring factions in the valleys and townships of KwaZulu-Natal or the areas around Johannesburg. Mandela was on a shortening fuse as violence escalated, with dozens of people dying almost daily.

Mandela addressed a closed-door meeting of United States Congress members and their aides in Cape Town on 3 April, during which he delivered a tirade against De Klerk for the continuing violence. The following day he told the ANC National Executive Committee meeting that he had been wrong to call De Klerk a 'man of integrity'. And so it was no surprise that the next day the ANC delivered a public ultimatum giving De Klerk until 9 May to take seven steps to end violence or talks would cease.

The peace process approached collapse when, on 19 July, newspapers published details showing the government had helped fund Inkatha, including giving it money for rallies held in November 1988 and March 1989. Newspapers said they had evidence that government was supplying Inkatha with guns and giving military training to its cadres.

Foreign Minister Pik Botha held a press conference, which was carefully edited before being broadcast, at South African Broadcasting Corporation television studios. During this conference journalists accused the government of duplicity and being involved in the murders of hundreds of civilians in KwaZulu-Natal. A sanguine Botha denied this (the TRC subsequently showed that the allegations were true) and dismissed the accusations of journalists as hysterical propaganda.

Tensions continued to rise. On 14 September, a national peace conference was held in Johannesburg, convened by church groups and civil society. This was the first face-to-face meeting of Mandela, De Klerk and Buthelezi on one platform. Their unhappy faces in photographs reflect the mood, portending the failure of the meeting. A Peace Accord was drawn up and signed by all parties, but it might as well have been in invisible ink for the commitment those signatures carried. Civil society had, however, made its will known: it wanted talks to continue, it needed peace to prevail.

From 28 to 29 November, 60 delegates from 20 parties held talks at a hotel near Johannesburg International Airport (now OR Tambo International) to lay the ground rules for multiparty talks. The Pan Africanist Congress walked out on the second day.

OPPOSITE: Mandela travels through the streets of London with Queen Elizabeth II during a state visit in 1996.

Hopes that the Christmas season might bring goodwill proved unrealistic. The Convention for a Democratic South Africa (Codesa), which was supposed to be the very first phase of negotiations, began on 20 December with 18 delegations and government. Buthelezi refused to attend but sent delegates. Everyone was tired, tense and angry. De Klerk spoke at the end of the first session, saying government was not against an interim multiracial government and that power-sharing could be considered.

But he went on to question the ANC's right to participate in the convention by saying the ANC had not declared the whereabouts of its secret arms caches and was maintaining a private army. A visibly angry Mandela strode to the podium as De Klerk stepped off it. Mandela said the Nationalists were pursuing a double agenda by talking peace while 'conducting a war'. He added that De Klerk was 'not fit to be president'. Matters did not improve. The initial Codesa talks were relatively brief, and were succeeded by bilateral talks.

On 17 March, after a major defeat in a by-election in Potchefstroom for the National Party, De Klerk called a referendum on his policies. There was a huge turnout at the polls, and 68.6 percent of the all-white voters showed their support of negotiations.

However, the optimism the results engendered was soon dashed by the Boipatong massacre we read about in the previous chapter, where 46 people were massacred. The ANC suspended all political contacts with the government; those who sought war on both sides were justifiably pleased.

But efforts for peace came from unexpected quarters: on 16 November, Judge Goldstone announced that his commission had conducted an unprecedented raid on military intelligence's covert operations centre. His staff carried out boxes of files before astonished, and powerless military officials; Goldstone had struck at the heart of the cobra that defended apartheid. In those files his officials found data about state involvement in assassinations and the covert fomenting of violence. De Klerk appointed the Steyn Commission, which, a month later, suspended or retired 23 officers, but this was seen as an exercise in damage control and of little import; the strength of the military had already been sapped by a process toward democracy that they no longer had real ability to derail.

On 12 February 1993 the ANC and government announced an agreement in principle on a five-year transition. During this transition, a Government of National Unity, formed by the main election winners, would govern. On 5 March Codesa talks resumed. Delegates burned the midnight oil as they raced toward a 1994 election date. They were still leaping countless

I was wrong to call FW de Klerk a man of integrity.

Nelson Mandela
To the ANC National Executive Committee
meeting, 4 April 1991

RIGHT: Right-wing South Africans show their fear of change in December 1991.

124

hurdles, particularly those imposed by right-wing bombings and killings. Codesa held its third plenary session on 1 April, with 25 parties participating, including the white right-wing Conservative Party. Right-wing thugs drove an armoured vehicle into the multiparty talks centre, making an aggressive, but ultimately futile, threat.

What had a more profound effect, however, was the assassination on 10 April of the most popular man in the ANC, the South African Communist Party Secretary-General and former MK leader, Chris Hani. He, who had gone out of his way to reconcile, was murdered in the driveway of his home by Janus Walusz, a right-wing Polish immigrant, in conspiracy with Conservative Party MP Clive Derby-Lewis. Hani's 15-year-old daughter, Nomakwezi, ran outside to find her father fatally wounded; she too would die tragically of an asthma attack a few years later. A white neighbour spotted the getaway vehicle and called the police, and Walusz was arrested a short

distance away. Hani's best friend, Tokyo Sexwale, rushed to the family home and newspapers around the world saw him sobbing over his friend's covered body. But Sexwale led those calling for peace and solidarity. The turmoil the right wing hoped would result never happened as ANC leaders appealed for calm and disciplined behaviour. Hani's death saw profound mourning nationwide.

More sadness was in store for the ANC and the nation. Fourteen days later, Oliver Tambo, president of the ANC from 1967 to 1991 (when Mandela was elected president of the ANC), died of a stroke. He was 75; his two daughters, son and his wife, Adelaide, were with him as he passed on. If anything, these two blows firmed Mandela's resolve and that of the ANC: there was no time to waste.

In the final days of apartheid South Africa seemed to sink into mayhem. Opportunistic political alliances flourished. A Freedom Alliance was formed between Inkatha and right-wing Afrikaners, war talk abounded, and Afrikaners threatened to secede from South Africa. Sixty-nine towns, in what was then the Transvaal (and what would later become the provinces of Gauteng and Mpumalanga), and 50 towns and villages elsewhere, extending in a sickle down the centre of the country, declared themselves *Volkstate* (people's states), in an attempt to create independent Afrikaner homelands.

Standerton (located in present-day Mpumalanga), a town of 15,000 whites and 65,000 blacks that was ruled by white councillors, called itself a *Volkstaat* in November 1993. In response, it was crippled by a black consumer boycott of the town's businesses. The town cleaved. Whites walked around with side-arms strapped to their waists in holsters and black people joined the militant anti-white PAC. When white businesspeople realised the boycott was destroying them financially, they began pressurising for change. One Standerton

LEFT: A rare sign of friendship between Nelson Mandela and FW de Klerk during the Codesa talks.

businessman complained that he had lost the contract for a R11-million factory to be put up by foreign investors when they realised Standerton had called itself a *Volkstaat*. And in yet more symptoms of what appeared to be growing anarchy, Bophuthatswana (a black homeland) threatened to declare unilateral independence, as did KwaZulu-Natal under Buthelezi.

And through it all there seemed no end to barbarity; an attempt by right-wing militarists to create problems in Bophuthatswana saw three of them executed by Bophuthatswana militia as they lay begging for mercy at a roadside. Mandela's soft demeanour and ready smile became sad, even though freedom seemed so close.

The first democratic election held in South Africa, in 1994, was beset with flaws. There was chaos in many areas of the country on the ballot days, as violent elements attempted to sway voters or intimidate them into staying away from the polls. Ballot papers arrived late in some parts

OPPOSITE: Mandela, carrier of hopes, implementer of dreams.

BELOW: Mandela is surrounded by a throng of people in an election campaign visit to Khayelitsha, Cape Town, in September 1993.

PREVIOUS PAGES: Some 40,000 ANC supporters listen to Mandela in Mmabatho in March 1994, ahead of the democratic elections.

OPPOSITE: Mandela casts his vote on 26 April 1994.

BELOW: The first day of the 1994 election was marked by an enthusiastic turnout at the polls. Despite standing for hours in long queues, voters reported the atmosphere as festive.

of the country, in others electoral officials forgot to send ink, but there was a profound commitment to show the world that even though there was disarray, this election would be pulled off, on time, and fairly.

The first day of elections, for pregnant women and for the elderly, was 26 April 1994. In the rural regions of KwaZulu-Natal, elderly people, when asked where they had come from, would look towards the blue hills on the distant horizon and say they had walked for two, or even three, days. Most were barefoot, some had a single shoe. They sat in the hot sun, without water, food or ablution facilities, patiently waiting to cast the first vote of their lifetime. Some slept in the open air under the cold night skies waiting for the polling booths to open the following day. Nothing was more precious than this first, centuries-elusive vote.

After several long days, during which the ballot papers were counted, Nelson Rolihlahla Mandela, who had himself voted for the first time ever at the age of 75, was elected the president of South Africa.

On 10 May 1994, Mandela was inaugurated as president with Thabo Mbeki and FW de Klerk as his deputy presidents. Six thousand delegates from around the world attended the ceremony, including Britain's Prince Philip, the Duke of Edinburgh, and Palestine's Yasser Arafat. It was the largest gathering of international heads of state since the funeral of John F Kennedy in 1963. For South Africans the time of deepest emotion came not when Mandela made his pledges as president, but when the Air Force flew by in salute. Six helicopters bore the new flag; the military had finally bowed to democracy.

We must work for the day when we, as South Africans, see one another and interact with one another as equal human beings and as part of one nation united, rather than torn asunder, by its diversity. All of us know how stubbornly racism can cling to the mind and how deeply it can infect the human soul.

Nelson Mandela
Address to the United Nations General
Assembly, New York,
3 October 1994

LEFT: Mandela, during the presidential inauguration ceremony, 10 May 1994.

In his inaugural address Mandela spoke of the 'human disaster' of apartheid. 'We saw our country tear itself apart in terrible conflict ... The time for healing of wounds has come ... Never, never again will this beautiful land experience the oppression of one by another.'

Urging forgiveness and reconciliation, he said in Afrikaans, the predominant language of his former enemies: '*Wat is verby, verby*' (what is past, is past).

Within three months violence was a distant memory. Government presented the plans of an ambitious vision to ensure greater equity among all: the Reconstruction and Development

In the presence of those assembled here, and in the full realisation of the high calling I assume as executive President in the service of the Republic of South Africa, I, Nelson Rolihlahla Mandela, do hereby swear to be faithful to the Republic of South Africa, and do solemnly and sincerely promise at all times to promote that which will advance, and oppose all that may harm the Republic, to obey, observe, uphold and maintain the Constitution and all other laws of the Republic, to discharge my duties with all my strength and talents to the best of my knowledge and ability and, true to the dictates of my conscience, to do justice to the well-being of the Republic and all its people. So help me God.

Nelson Mandela
Taking the oath of office, 10 May 1994.

Programme. Government also announced a Truth and Reconciliation Commission to investigate death squads, but many criticised its far-reaching amnesty clauses. However, Mandela insisted that these amnesty clauses were essential to get perpetrators to confess, and through that process for families to find healing in finally learning what had happened to their loved ones.

More black families moved into wealthy, previously white, neighbourhoods. Black entrepreneurs set up stands on the sidewalks of suburbs where they would never before have dreamed of establishing a business. Hope had finally come home to South Africa.

As invariably happens when the time comes to gather the harvest, many have appeared in our midst who claim that they, and not the millions who sustained the struggle for many decades under the leadership of the ANC, are the ones who planted the seed and tended the tree of freedom.

Nelson Mandela
8 January 1996 statement

RIGHT: A serious Mandela goes over his notes prior to a 1994 televison debate with FW de Klerk in the days leading up to South Africa's first democratic elections.

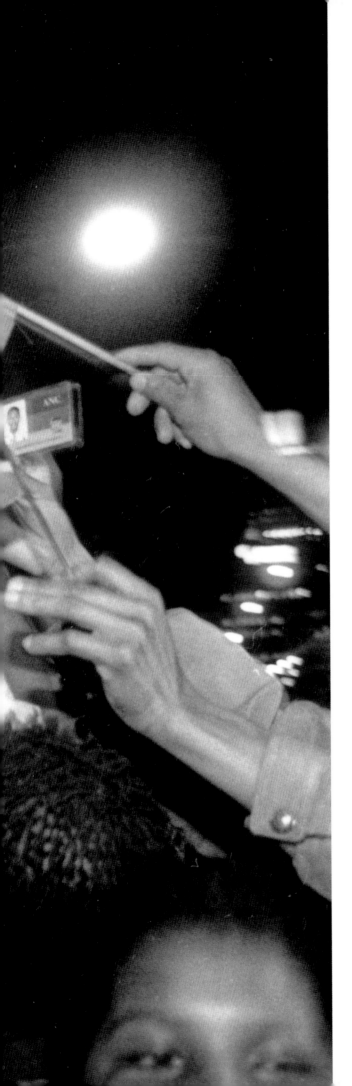

At the end goodwill prevailed

At the end, the bloodletting stopped. At the end, goodwill prevailed. At the end, the overwhelming majority, both black and white, decided to invest in peace.

President Nelson Mandela
To the Joint Houses of the Congress of the United States of America,
6 October 1994

IN A TRIBUTE to President Mandela, the day before his eightieth birthday in 1998, *The Monitor*, the premier newspaper of Kampala, Uganda, wrote: 'There is no known accolade which has not been bestowed upon Mandela.' Africans loved the way he brought honour to an oft-maligned continent. He brought dignity to people discouraged by too often being seen as having a begging bowl in one hand and a Kalashnikov in the other. And so his success was shared.

The Monitor continued: 'Mandela said he would serve one term, and he is living up to his word. Last year, he chose to hand over the leadership of the ruling ANC to his heir-apparent Thabo Mbeki. Next year he is set to leave the presidency. He has already relinquished most of the functions of the office. In South Africa itself, Mandela's rule has brought its share of disappointments. Crime is still rampant. Promises of economic empowerment and housing for millions of black South Africans who were victims of apartheid have not been met, and the people are angry and feeling let down. But dismantling the legacy of apartheid, and making all the blacks rich could not have been Mandela's main job. Mandela showed that it was possible to rise beyond the politics of hate, race, and that any price is worth paying for a democracy.'

And so Mandela found that his help was often sought to bring peace, and hopefully, democracy, to a turbulent continent. As an example, in August 1998 when Zimbabwe, Angola and Namibia went to war against Uganda and Rwanda, on the side of the Democratic Republic of Congo's then President Laurent Kabila, Mandela, as chairman of the Southern African Development Community (SADC), spent long days and nights trying to broker peace. After the first weekend a ceasefire was announced, but war again broke out in a region that has not seen stability for more than four decades. It was one of the many conflicts that then and now crush the hopes for peace and growth in Africa.

The evocative words spoken almost a century before, in 1882, by one of the founders of the Native National Congress (later the ANC), the Reverend John L Dube, rang as true then as now.

What characterises his presidency is his human touch and sensitivity toward the disadvantaged and not in a racial way. He is as sensitive to a white child with leukaemia as he is to a township child who has been raped, or whose sibling has been murdered.

Jay Naidoo
(Former Minister of Posts, Telecommunications and Broadcasting)

PREVIOUS PAGES: Black South Africans show their joy after the 1994 ANC election victory.

RIGHT: Mandela adores women and they him. Here, on one of his informal neighbourhood walkabouts he is greeted by residents of a housing complex.

May 1994

He wrote, 'Oh! How I long for that day when darkness and gloom shall have passed away because the Sun of Righteousness has risen with healing in His hand. This shall be the dawning of a brighter day for the people of Africa.'

Those words were echoed again in 1906, by Pixley kaIsaka Seme, who would lead the NNC, when he wrote of the 'regeneration of Africa' and said 'the demon of racialism, the aberrations of the Xhosa-Fingo feud, the animosity that exists between the Zulus and the Tongas, between the Basutos and every other native must be buried and forgotten: it has shed among us sufficient

ABOVE: Former United States president
Bill Clinton and Mandela have
developed a genuinely caring friendship.

OPPOSITE: Mandela reads the
newspaper at his home.

blood. We are one people. These divisions, these jealousies, are the cause of all our woes and of all our backwardness and ignorance today.'

His call was repeated by Thabo Mbeki after he became president in 1999, when he too spoke of the 'regeneration of Africa'. But Mbeki, like Seme before him, did not match words with practice. By the end of his second term in office – when he was all but kicked out by an angry ANC – more than 350,000 people had died needlessly of AIDS, according to Harvard University, because he refused to issue anti-retroviral medication to help extend their lives. He oversaw the most prosperous period in sixty years when he was president, but it had less to do with his rule than with a global economic boom, which was followed in 2008 by one of the worst financial crisisses the world has seen.

Mandela recognised that reconciliation meant extending a hand first to one's enemies: trying to understand and allay their fears and bring them into the circle of one's friends, making them understand that the most difficult task had to be accomplished first – negotiating peace with a foe. He often faltered and failed; some of his dealings with De Klerk were petulant rather than statesmanlike, but as he oft reminds us, he is a man, not a saint.

Terror Lekota, ANC chairman for a decade from December 1997, reflected: 'Mandela won over the international community to give maximum support to this fledgling democracy. From the point of view of superpowers, we needed the friendship of countries like the USA and Britain, but not at any cost. Nelson created a place for South Africa as a model of conflict resolution and … as international advocates of peace. His intervention in the Democratic Republic of Congo, in Indonesia, and then Ireland and the Angolan conflict were examples of his role as peacemaker, and a recognition of South Africans, with their negotiating skills as peace brokers.

'Although we had an alliance with the South African Communist Party we were not against a market economy, we became committed to it. Mandela went to South Africa's business community and made a huge impact on them, swinging them around to be supportive of this government in a manner very few could have done.'

Mandela, like Britain's wartime premier Winston Churchill, was the right man at the right time and with the correct instincts. But he did not always succeed when it came to managing his robust, and sometimes corrupt, family, and he was not always an astute governor. He failed to pay much attention to HIV and AIDS until it took the life of his son, Makgatho, and other family members, and even though he did not like Mbeki and said he would have preferred Cyril Ramaphosa as his successor, he allowed Mbeki to ruthlessly shoulder away other potential leaders for the 1999 presidency. Mandela's greatest value – more even than helping conquer apartheid – was in the love he gave to a bruised nation. He gave his opponents reason to feel safe in territory that they, too, had considered hostile before.

Sheila Camerer, a leading parliamentarian first of the National Party and later of the liberal Democratic Alliance (DA), said of Mandela, 'He is the only president I have known around parliament who never rushed by ordinary MPs smiling and waving. He always stopped and took trouble to greet you personally. It must have been hell for the minders who [were] trying to get him to the next meeting.' She recalls an early evening function when she was sworn in as Deputy Minister in Mandela's government of National Unity: '… my mother, who has difficulty walking, also attended. After the ceremony everyone moved through to the next room where cocktails and snacks were served and a string quartet was playing. My mother, who had been sitting in a corner somehow got left out of the general move, which he [Mandela] spotted. He went across and gave her his arm and escorted her through to the party, which of course left her an undying admirer.'

Mac Maharaj reflects: 'Before and after April 1994 we felt his deep sense of genuine empathy and concern about the people of this country, including white people, for which he was criticised for reaching out the hand of reconciliation too far. Children have a keener sense of his genuine humility and warmth. Wherever he goes, they swamp him while their parents are more intimidated by the imposing stature of a great man. He rejoices in the joy of others. This is the secret behind his sunshine smile. It's part of his hands-on approach to everything. It's the intuitive feel that doesn't require image consultants and publicity agents.'

Mandela led by example, speaking again and again of the 'great importance to assert the primacy of social morality among our people'. He said this morality needed to 'form part of a new patriotism which should inspire and motivate the majority of our people'. It needed to combat

True reconciliation does not consist in merely forgetting the past. It does not rest with black forgiveness, sensitivity to white fears and tolerance of an unjust status quo on one hand, and white gratitude and appreciation underlined by a tenacious clinging to exclusive privilege on the other. It has to be based on the creation of a truly democratic, nonracial and nonsexist society.

Nelson Mandela
ANC Conference, 1997

lawlessness, corruption, terror, and disregard for the norms of a just and equitable society: '... we must continue the struggle to give life to what we said in the Freedom Charter – that South Africa belongs to all who live in it, black and white, and that no government can justly claim authority unless it is based on the will of the people as a whole. But the national reconciliation for which we continue to struggle cannot be founded on the preservation and perpetuation of the old order of white privilege and black deprivation.

'True reconciliation does not consist in merely forgetting the past. It does not rest with black forgiveness, sensitivity to white fears and tolerance of an unjust status quo on one hand, and white gratitude and appreciation underlined by a tenacious clinging to exclusive privilege on the other. It has to be based on the creation of a truly democratic, nonracial and nonsexist society. A serious challenge faces our white compatriots to grasp fully the importance of their role in the efforts to achieve national reconciliation. ... Vengeance is not our goal. The building of a new nation at peace with itself because it is reconciled with its past is our objective.'

Speaking to the ANC's national conference in December 1997 Mandela said: 'We seek not just freedom but opportunity – not just legal equity but human ability – not just equality as a right and a theory, but equality as a fact and as a result. We have experienced serious resistance to the transformation of the public service, with representatives of the old order using all means in their power to ensure that they remain in dominant positions.'

Mandela was the president of reconciliation and peace. Maharaj recalls, 'We all remember his hand reaching out to FW de Klerk at the end of a tense harsh live TV debate in the run-up to the 1994 elections; his donning of the Springbok rugby No. 6 jersey at the World Cup Final [indeed this became the subject of a successful film by Clint Eastwood called *Invictus*]; his appearances in communities gripped by fear generated by violence as in Richmond and the Cape Flats; his visit to Betsie Verwoerd [the widow of apartheid's architect Hendrik Verwoerd] in Orania; his systematic and continuous reaching out to Mangosuthu Buthelezi; the phone call or the unexpected visit ... .

'Many who accompany him on his punishing schedule criss-crossing the length and breadth of South Africa on visits to communities come out exhausted, but he emerged energised and revitalised.' His 1994 election campaign schedule was so gruelling that the media assigned rotating teams after their young reporters complained of exhaustion.

But as he and the ANC began governing, it found divisions widening between itself and its followers. Maharaj, who would later become spokesperson for President Jacob Zuma in July 2011, reflected: 'The historic responsibilities placed on the ANC multiplied. Maintaining and continuously re-energising the ANC as the political instrument for mobilisation and transformation must now go side by side with the task of ensuring that the ANC in government ... draws together the entire nation-in-making into effecting transformation. By exhortation and his actions Madiba asks that we continuously deepen our links with the people.'

As the possibility of nations to become islands sufficient unto themselves diminishes and vanishes forever, so will it be that the suffering of the one shall, at the same time, inflict pain upon the other.

Nelson Mandela
To the United States Congress, 1994

BELOW: The Princess of Wales visited South Africa shortly before her death in 1997. As well as sharing a great love for children, she and President Mandela had a remarkable rapport.

Lekota agrees: 'Before we came to government we had only our organisation to service, now we have government too. We took a lot of our most experienced people and put them in government. We should have left some to continue running the organisation'.

The ANC may have battled to retain cohesion, but the gains made for ordinary South Africans were many. Mandela said in his address to the joint sitting of the United States Congress on 6 October 1994: 'The time that has passed has allowed me to come back to you to speak not of a dream deferred, of which your fellow countryman Langston Hughes spoke. The history that cannot be unmade has enabled me to repeat in this chamber the power of the triumph of the oppressed. For, as the representatives of centuries of white minority rule bowed to the results of the democratic process, the people did, as your fellow countryman, Martin Luther King, Jr, did, cry out: "Free at last, free at last, thank God Almighty we are free at last!" Both black and white in our country can say today we are

ABOVE: Dressed in a South African cricket blazer and cap, the President congratulates cricketer Adrian Kuiper after the South Africa/New Zealand match at Port Elizabeth on 22 January 1996.

OPPOSITE: President Mandela with a victorious Bafana Bafana captain Neil Tovey at the African Cup of Nations soccer tournament in 1996.

brother and sister to one another, a united rainbow nation that derives its strength from the bonding of its many races and colours, constitutes a celebration of the oneness of the human race.'

In his last speech at the opening of parliament in February 1998 in Cape Town, Mandela reflected on the gains that had been made for ordinary people, and how they could be mobilised 'to be their own liberators'. He pointed to successes: 'Last year, we increased the supply of clean and accessible water from 700,000 to 1.3 million South Africans. We surpassed our plans to build or upgrade 500 clinics last year. The primary school feeding scheme reaches 4.9 million children. We will make 421,000 telephone connections this year. In 1997 we made 400,000 electricity connections, meaning South Africa has reached a 58 percent electrification level. The law on secure land tenure will bring more certainty into the lives of over six million citizens. We are at the beginning of an arduous and protracted struggle for a better quality of life. In the course of this struggle, we shall have immediate successes; we shall have setbacks; but we shall progress, inch by inch, towards our goal. Measures to eliminate corruption have uncovered many fraudsters in the government machinery. Some public servants are, to put it mildly, not imbued with the spirit of public service. Even in instances where funds are available, they do not turn up on time or they relate to senior citizens with attitudes bordering on the criminal.'

One of Mandela's key cabinet ministers, Jay Naidoo, said, 'We had to work within the constraints of a government designed to deal with the needs of a small minority. Transformation in terms of policies, laws and institutions, budgets, civil service and delivery mechanisms, all constitutes governance. How do you deliver in an innovative and creative way and transform orthodoxy to revolutionary? We had to transform the way we deliver services – citizens are the main customers of government – we had to change the culture and value system. You must not underestimate transition. It was bold, courageous and risky. Obviously the charisma of Mandela has been important but what underpinned that were a set of circumstances that were a compromise.

'We did not win a military victory, it was a compromise.

'We reshaped policies, strategies and delivery systems. We [tried] to revitalise the civil service and transform its leadership. We have to get the culture right so that civil servants know they are there to deliver to the people. We have too much on paper and not enough in practice.'

Mandela's advances in extending social justice and opportunity to all would not be matched by those who succeeded him in power; government would become the largest creator of jobs, and those who found work would be overpaid and overprotected by unions. Joblessness deepened with complex labour laws dissuading employers from employing any more than necessary. However, medical services, even though they are eroding, remain better than in many developed nations and are free, which in certain advanced nations, like the United States, they are not. South Africa is significantly more advanced in technology than many developed nations; its mobile telephony is more reliable than in the United States and its roads are often better maintained. But those who succeeded Mandela in power failed to carefully govern, leading to ongoing protests for 'delivery' of the most basic services, whether safe schools, homes that do not collapse, sanitation or even street cleaning.

Naidoo said then: 'The question is not vision, it is strategy. Mandela has been an anchor for stabilising the transition, his status, charisma, his warmth, his

BELOW: President Mandela proudly donned a Springbok Number 6 jersey when he awarded the World Cup trophy to rugby captain Francois Pienaar in 1995.

humility and the sacrifice that he made without being embittered was a very important anchor not just for us, but especially for whites and Afrikaners. He had visionary leadership that emphasised reconciliation.

'When we were being criticised by militants in our own ranks that we were overdoing reconciliation, he said: "What does it cost for us to reconcile? What is taking money from our government to meet the needs of the white minority? The most significant slice of budgetary resources is toward closing the development gap with health, education and telephones." And people had no answer to that. His leadership has been important, even though he has not been correct all the time.

'One of the most exciting periods of our history has been the last 50 years of struggle and the most exciting period the first five years of [democratic] government. It inspired people and made them part of rebuilding.'

In his speech to the United States Congress on 6 October 1994, President Mandela underpinned the challenge of the millennium to come, when he said: 'As we look and look again at the reality that freedom brings, we see together with TS Eliot that we are, still:

ABOVE: Mandela celebrates South Africa winning the 2010 Fifa World Cup bid in Zurich, with soccer boss Danny Jordaan and a jubilant Archbishop Desmond Tutu in the background, and Irvin Khoza to the right.

> *In the uncertain hour before the morning*
> *Near the ending of interminable night*
> *At the recurrent end of the unending ...*
> *While the dead leaves still rattled on like tin*
> *Over the asphalt where no other sound was.*

The rattle of leaves was a symbol for the echo of poverty, the '... pervasive poverty that afflicts our society; the despair of millions who are without jobs and without hope; the unborn who we know will be born disabled and die before their maturity because of poverty; the darkness that engulfs millions because they are illiterate and innumerate; the many who will be victims of rape, robbery and other violent crimes because hunger, want and brutalisation have warped and condemned many a human soul ... The new age will surely demand that democracy must also mean a life of plenty.

'As the images of life lived anywhere on our globe become available to all, so will the contrast between the rich and the poor within and across frontiers, and within and across the continents, become a motivating force impelling the deprived to demand a better life from the powers that be, whatever their location.

'As the possibility of nations to become islands, sufficient unto themselves, diminishes and vanishes forever, so will it be that the suffering of the one shall, at the same time, inflict pain upon the other.'

The rainbow nation loses its pot of gold

'The President of the Republic should promote the unity of the nation and that which will advance the Republic.'

South African Constitution

DURING HIS PRESIDENCY Mandela was aware of widespread fears about 'what will happen after Mandela goes', and of the potentially damaging economic implications of such fears. Halfway into his five-year term of office, Mandela began shifting responsibility for the day-to-day running of government to his deputy, Thabo Mbeki.

Mandela even delivered a controversial speech, drafted by Mbeki, to the ANC conference in December 1997. It attacked the media, whites for failing to reform, and international donors for not upholding their promises – it was torn apart by critics. Why did Mandela read a speech he knew would be widely criticised? According to a senior ANC official: 'Mandela was not happy with the speech, although he agreed with some of its content. But he also knew that if Mbeki delivered a speech like that it would cause him and the country grave damage, but because of Mandela's stature the speech could be carried off – still with the harshest criticism of Mandela's presidency, but without causing damage to the economy.'

That view is moot, as others claimed Mandela considered it better for Mbeki to learn through mistakes Mandela could carry than for a new president to founder on ill-considered words. If so, it was a patronising and inadvisable step because this was not a lesson Mbeki learnt, as his later actions would show.

The notion of Mbeki as crown prince was a deliberate strategy of Oliver Tambo; although he had a son, Dali, Tambo took Mbeki under his wing and groomed him from the time the young man went into exile (Dali was at least a decade and a half younger than Thabo and showed no interest in politics then or later). Not all were happy with this. At the National Executive Committee meeting of the ANC in Lusaka on Friday, 27 October 1989, the minutes record intelligence commissar, Joe

Nhlanhla, saying: 'I'm concerned that the media are harping on the issue of the Crown Prince [Thabo Mbeki]. We can treat such matters as nonsense but people ask us about them ...'.

And so it was that the election of Thabo Mbeki was almost a foregone conclusion, and when some – like Cyril Ramaphosa, Mac Maharaj or Tokyo Sexwale – showed an interest in the post, or supporters tried to promote their election, Mbeki ruthlessly conspired to render any opposition to his bid redundant. Mandela presented the choice of Ramaphosa and Mbeki to three ANC senior officials – Walter Sisulu, Thomas Nkobi and Jacob Zuma. They unanimously said, 'It must be Mbeki', even after Mandela stated his preference for then trade union leader and now businessman Ramaphosa. Indeed, Cyril was the man the nation wanted, but in the end ANC exile politics were triumphant.

Mandela also consulted with senior alliance partners (those in the Congress of South Africa Trade Unions and the South African Communist Party) and, in a meeting with trade unionists John Gonomo and Mbhazima Shilowa and South African Communist Party heads Joe Slovo and Charles Nqakula, only Slovo declared himself against Mbeki.

Govan Mbeki appeared strangely ambivalent. Govan, one of Mandela's oldest friends, but, too, the friend most likely to take issue with Mandela, was asked what he believed would be the differences in the presidential styles of his son, Thabo Mbeki, and Mandela. 'The difference,' he finally said, 'is that Nelson is tall, and Thabo is short.' In hindsight it was a telling comment that referred to more than physique; it spoke too of depth of vision and ability to lead. To commentators then it sounded like an amusing quip, but Govan, who had strained relations with his elder son, was never one for a thoughtless comment.

LEFT: Thabo Mbeki with his wife Zanele.

OPPOSITE (LEFT TO RIGHT): Mandela's preferred presidential candidate for 1999 was Cyril Ramaphosa, although his bid for the presidency was thwarted by Thabo Mbeki; rarely to the fore publicly, accomplished lawyer Mathews Phosa is nevertheless one of the most powerful political figures in South Africa; and Tokyo Sexwale, successful businessman and cabinet minister, failed in his presidential quest, losing to Jacob Zuma, who was elected in 2009.

PREVIOUS PAGES: United States First Lady Michelle Obama meets with Mandela at his home in Houghton, Johannesburg.

He added, in the formal manner of the Rivonia Trialists: 'He's a highly intelligent young man who I believe will not do anything stupid.' However, by the end of his second term in office Thabo Mbeki was so universally disliked in South Africa and in the ANC that at an ANC conference in Polokwane on 16 December 2007, he suffered a crushing series of boos and jeers that led to his defeat. No senior politician had ever been so publicly humiliated in South Africa.

Mbeki senior, who would die in August 2001, confessed in long interviews with me, that he never really knew his son: 'He was 19 when he went into exile and I went to jail.' Indeed, an impassioned speech by Thabo to the United Nations Special Committee Against Apartheid a short while after he went into exile may have helped deter the apartheid government from placing a noose around the necks of Govan, Mandela and their fellow Rivonia Trialists.

However, by June 1999, during Thabo's first speech to parliament after being elected president, Govan was so excited he could barely contain himself. His wife, Epainette, Thabo's mother, sat to his left, dressed in black, her demeanour severe and unsmiling. Close by, Thabo's wife, Zanele, sat on her own in a peach suit, among a row of empty seats.

As Mbeki shuffled his papers before and during the address he looked up at his parents, almost in the way a schoolboy will look to his parents for assurance. Govan almost leapt up he was so thrilled: Epainette and Zanele remained impassive. Thabo would look up at them occasionally during his speech, and while Epainette remained inscrutable, Govan would applaud some statements, his hands fluttering in excitement. That brief cameo spoke volumes about the child who was groomed to be president and the coldness he experienced from his mother, the only parent left at home while his father was jailed.

The apartness of those family members closest to Mbeki told their own tale of a man whose presidency was marked by a solitary disdain of the people he governed, and an apparent inability to empathise. But in many other ways Mbeki was blessed: his family was part of an intellectual elite and he grew up for most of his late childhood and adolescence in the home of Michael Muendane; there neither love nor opportunity were limited. As a young man Mbeki's diplomacy also very quickly saw him attain powerful positions in the exiled ANC.

While Mbeki lacked the quiet wisdom of Tambo, or the good cheer of Mandela, he used the ceremony marking the unveiling of the South African constitution to reveal a passionate heart behind his stiff façade. On 8 May 1996, in the stuffy confines of the small Constituent Assembly at Cape Town's parliament, he delivered a speech that left few dry eyes in the house:

'I am an African.

'I owe my being to the hills and the valleys, the mountains and the glades, the rivers, the deserts, the trees, the flowers, the seas and the ever-changing seasons that define the face of our native land.

'My body has frozen in our frosts; it has thawed in the warmth of our sunshine. I owe my being to the Khoi and the San whose desolate souls haunt the great expanses of the beautiful Cape – they who fell victim to the most merciless genocide our native land has ever seen; the first to lose their lives in the struggle to defend our freedom …

'I am formed of the migrants who left Europe to find a new home on our native land. Whatever their own actions, they remain still, part of me … All this I know and know to be true because I am an African!'

Then, in a voice that rose and fell with the meaning of his words, he said: 'I am a nation that would not allow that fear of death, torture, imprisonment, exile or persecution should result in the perpetuation of injustice …

'The constitution whose adoption we celebrate constitutes an unequivocal statement that we refuse to accept that our Africanness shall be defined by our

BELOW: Queen Beatrix of the Netherlands accompanies Mandela through St Pieters Church in Leiden, not long after his release.

race, colour, gender or historical origins; South Africa belongs to all who live in it, black and white … It seeks to create the situation in which all our people shall be free from fear.

'It rejoices in the diversity of our people and creates the space for all of us voluntarily to define ourselves as one people … Whatever the setbacks of the moment, nothing can stop us now! Whatever the difficulties, Africa shall be at peace! However improbable it may sound to the sceptics, Africa will prosper!'

Mbeki spoke with a beauty and poetry that Mandela's monotonous speech delivery could never match. But, while Mandela's heart appears in his actions and a smile is often in his eyes, some said Mbeki's words were poetry devoid of emotion. His rhetoric inspired but the will to implement was missing.

Mandela focused on a peaceful revolution among his people and conquered the world. Mbeki believed that, by pushing for African growth and development, South Africa could extend its markets. The concept of an African union is good but is rendered difficult to implement by a lack of shared airspace, crumbling rail infrastructure and poor roads across the continent, not to mention frequent wars and conflict. During Mbeki's presidency a black elite broadened and became entrenched, but wage gaps widened, and unemployment and poverty deepened.

Mbeki's controversial stance on HIV and AIDS – questioning whether HIV caused AIDS, and courting dissidents – saw South Africa carry the highest number of infected people in the world. In 2002, 600,000 South Africans died of the disease. In 2003 the courts forced Mbeki, who had thus far refused, to extend AIDS medication to those ill with HIV, but by then it was too late for many. UNAIDS estimated that AIDS claimed 310,000 lives in 2009 – almost 850 every day.

But in fairness, when Mandela was president he too did little to combat HIV. However, by 2000 the impact of the virus was being felt by Mandela: he lost relatives to HIV, and talked of some of his bursary holders who came to him desperately ill with the virus – only to stage dramatic turnarounds when he paid for their antiretroviral care.

He and Mbeki began publicly contradicting each other on HIV and AIDS. The ANC backed Mbeki and upbraided Mandela for openly calling for antiretroviral treatment for HIV. Mandela ignored them; in 2002 he sat on the stage at the Barcelona World AIDS Conference with former United States president Bill Clinton and other world leaders, calling on presidents and governments to act with urgency to combat the fatal scourge.

But Mbeki was seen as a person not to trifle with. Talk among parliamentarians was legendary of how he would insult and castigate those who dared question him.

In 2000, *Sunday Times* journalists Carol Paton and Mondli Makhanya described Mbeki's government thus: 'Policy co-ordination and implementation are now tightly controlled from his office, and all directors-general [of the various ministries] report to [the Reverend] Frank Chikane, the director-general of the presidency … The core ideas and even phrases in Mbeki's parliamentary speeches have been echoed by ANC MPs and ministers on hundreds of occasions

– illustrating, on the one hand, a disturbing sign of the tendency among party members to agree sycophantically with the president.'

An excess of control from the centre saw the energy and innovation of Mandela's presidency disappear. Protocol ruled as imagination waned.

After Mbeki's removal from power by the ANC, Jacob Zuma, who had orchestrated much of the anti-Mbeki sentiment at Polokwane, was elected president. His election was controversial; a polygamist, he has fathered 22 children, some with his wives and others with girlfriends. In 2005 he was acquitted of the rape of a young HIV-positive family friend, and in 2009, the National Prosecuting Authority, citing 'political pressure', dropped charges of corruption against him relating to allegations centring around South Africa's scandal-ridden multi-million-rand arms deal of 1999.

Zuma's years as president have been beset with serious claims of corruption, racketeering and even murder by top officials, including serious charges levelled against two police chiefs in a row. Multi-billionaire Brett

ABOVE: Mandela attends a 2009 election rally.

Kebble, as an example, was shot dead by mafia gangsters who were closely linked to then police chief, Jackie Selebi, who was convicted of corruption and accepting bribes from a drug dealer. Then in July 2011, Public Protector Thuli Madonsela was threatened with arrest after announcing five months earlier that the R500-million lease on police headquarters was signed unlawfully. She said the accounting officer, South African Police commissioner General Bheki Cele, was among those responsible – he was later suspended by Zuma. She also criticised Public Works Minister Gwen Mahlangu-Nkabinde for going ahead with the deal in spite of legal advice against it.

In October 2011, Zuma sacked Mahlangu-Nkabinde and Cooperative Governance and Traditional Affairs Minister Sicelo Shiceka, who was also the focus of corruption allegations.

Under Zuma, governance became chaotic and factionalised. Professor Kwandiwe Kondlo of the University of the Free State also claimed that political appointments were tribally influenced, a dangerous charge in Africa. The ANC Youth League, which Mandela had once led, became angry and disruptive; the rhetoric of its leader, Julius Malema, was often racist and he threatened nationalisation of companies. Malema was convicted of sexism against a rape survivor, and yet another trial accused him of inciting racism; finally the ANC brought him before a disciplinary hearing after he insulted Botswana, but none of these actions deterred Malema. Privately Mandela was distressed, but his word no longer carried any weight. Publicly he was silent. It was an angry Archbishop Desmond Tutu who became the conscience of South Africa.

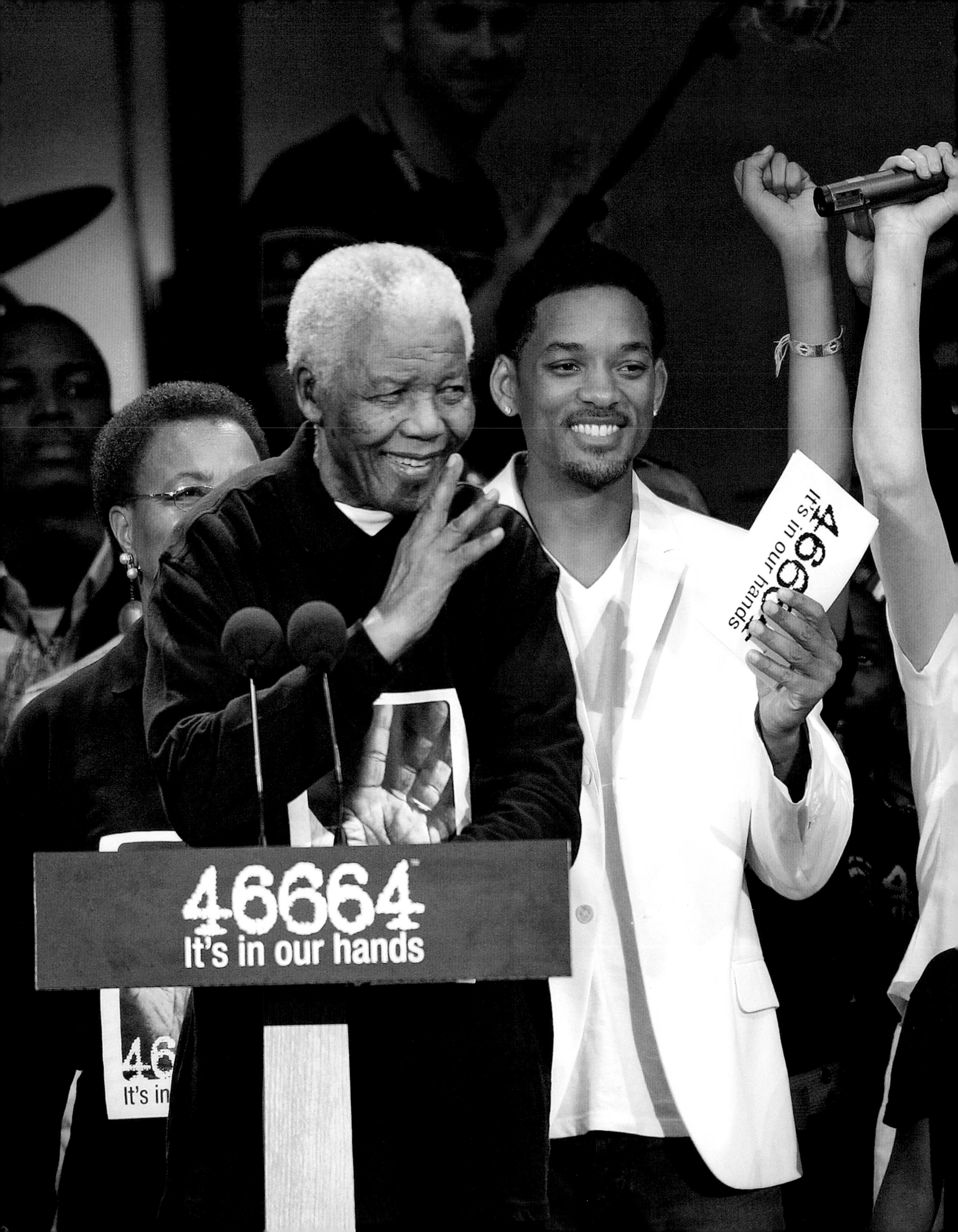
46664
It's in our hands
46664
It's in our hands

Siyabonga, Tata

Whatever my wishes might be, I cannot bind future generations to remember me in the particular way I would like. What always worried me in prison was [that I could acquire] the image of someone who is always 100 percent correct and can never do any wrong. People expect me to perform far beyond my ability.

Nelson Mandela

AFTER MANDELA LEFT THE PRESIDENCY he became involved in a range of issues: peace in central Africa, AIDS, and dozens of meetings with the world's talented and beautiful to lend support to his Children's Fund (and his own family). But prison taught Mandela to value seclusion, to have time to reflect, and his life after his release mirrored his prison existence in many ways. He would wake at 4.30 a.m., exercise for an hour (before the aches and pains of age made that more difficult) before taking a breakfast of porridge, fresh fruit and milk at 6.30 a.m. while he read the daily newspapers. He would then begin a full working day; this was often up to 12 hours long, but as the years passed he devoted increasing time to his large family.

Mandela loves few things more than to tell his grandchildren and great-grandchildren stories about his childhood, and the lessons he learnt as a boy. One of these was a lesson he applied as a political leader too: 'When you want to get a herd to move in a certain direction you stand at the back with a stick. Then a few of the more energetic cattle move to the front and the rest follow. That is how a leader should do his work.'

He tried to instil in his grandchildren and children the words he wrote to Winnie Mandela from Robben Island in 1975: 'Honesty, sincerity, simplicity, humility, pure generosity, absence of vanity, readiness to serve others – qualities which are within easy reach of every soul – are the foundation of one's spiritual life.' He would tell his family that thinking well of people sometimes makes them behave better than they would otherwise, and he would impress his own belief in the essential goodness of the human heart even when political governance in South Africa began lending to disappointment.

Mandela summed up the situation when he noted: 'The new conditions create temptations of self-interest and personal enrichment. Corruption, opportunism and self-serving careerism have no place in the organisation Walter Sisulu led and helped build.' Mandela's warnings about deepening poverty and the spread of disease have oft been ignored. Yet he has found it difficult to directly criticise the organisation for which he sacrificed so much.

He often stressed his belief in the value of a collective in decision-making – the importance of the people governing as Thomas Jefferson and Abraham Lincoln intended – but collectives are not always wise. And, if he no longer captained the team, Mandela had to anticipate that his criticisms would remain just that – they might give hope to citizens but do little to change policy within an organisation that has become increasingly intolerant of dissent.

Intolerance of the will of the people on the African continent was a challenge that perplexed him. He envisioned a role as a global peacemaker after he left the presidency, and so in 2000, not long after retiring, and following the death of the previous mediator, Tanzanian president Julius Nyerere, Mandela took on a role as chief mediator in the Burundi peace process. This followed devastating civil war and genocide based on tribal differences in the region. In May 2003, he witnessed the handover of power from Tutsi leader Pierre Buyoya to Domitien Ndayizeye, a Hutu, but achieving peace is hard, he would learn again and again.

That same year, Mandela made a rapid series of visits to Iran, Syria, Jordan, Israel, Gaza and the United States in a bid to broker a comprehensive Middle East peace. But despite what he described as 'positive and cordial' meetings with Israel's Prime Minister Ehud Barak and President Ezer Weizman, they rejected his offer of assistance.

If you have an objective in life, then you want to concentrate on that and not engage in infighting with your enemies. You want to create an atmosphere where you can move everybody towards the goal you have set for yourself.

Nelson Mandela

Nonetheless, he was heartened by the positive outcome of his interventions in East Timor, as well as the handing over by Libya of those accused of the bombing of the Pan Am flight over the Scottish town of Lockerbie in 1988 – that was the culmination of a seven-year mediation Mandela conducted with Saudi Arabia.

And then, within weeks of receiving the Presidential Medal of Freedom (the United States' highest civilian award) in December 2002, from President George Bush, Mandela laid into Bush for his threatening posture toward Iraq (which the United States and Britain invaded a few weeks later). Mandela accused Bush of coveting Iraq's oil. He referred to British Prime Minister Tony Blair as the 'foreign minister of the United States'. Mandela had overestimated his influence; when Bush visited South Africa in July 2003, the two avoided each other.

But, while the great and the famous may be able to intervene successfully in the workplace or even upon the world stage, the dynamics of personal relationships are always far more complicated.

Mandela's family as a whole lived lavishly and luxuriously, but few with the ostentation of Winnie and Zindzi – and 2003 was a bad year for both. In May the Johannesburg High Court ordered Zindzi to pay a bank more than R4 million that she had borrowed five years before to finance a South African tour by the famed American R&B group Boyz II Men.

In the same month Winnie and her financial advisor were found guilty in the Pretoria High Court of 'fraudulently obtaining loans of over $120,000 in the bogus names of African National Congress members'. She was sentenced to five years in prison with one year suspended, though she went on to appeal the verdict.

Mandela stayed far from these controversies, as he was consumed by grief; on 5 May he had been woken by his personal assistant, Zelda la Grange, and informed of the death of his closest friend and comrade, Walter Sisulu. Mandela had been staying at a luxurious game farm, where he was working on the sequel to his memoir *Long Walk to Freedom*. He dressed and returned to Johannesburg to give his condolences to Walter's wife, Albertina. Helped into the Sisulus' modest home in Johannesburg, the frail Mandela held the hands of the newly widowed Albertina and said, 'Xhamela is no more. May he live forever! A part of me is gone.'

Mandela spent two days with advisers working on his eulogy for Sisulu. He issued a media statement to the South African Press Association: 'During the past 62 years our lives have been intertwined. Together we forged common commitments. We walked side by side, nursing each other's bruises, holding each other up when our steps faltered. Together we savoured the taste of freedom.

'In a sense I feel cheated by Walter. If there be another life beyond this physical world I would have loved to be there first so that I could welcome him. I now know that when my time comes, Walter will be there to meet me, and I am almost certain he will hold out an enrolment form to register me into the ANC in that world, cajoling me with one of his favourite songs we sang when mobilising people behind the Freedom Charter:

ABOVE: Mandela attends the memorial service for his dear friend, the late Walter Sisulu.

OPPOSITE: Mandela arrives at the memorial service of his great-granddaughter, Zenani Mandela, in 2010.

PREVIOUS PAGES: Mandela speaks during the 46664 concert held in his honour in Hyde Park, London, in 2008. To his left are actor Will Smith and singer Annie Lennox.

*Libhaliwe na iGama lakho
kuloMqulu weNkululeko
Vuma silibhale kuloMqulu
weNkululeko.'*

(Has your name been enrolled in the struggle for freedom? Permit us to register you in the struggle for freedom.)

'I shall miss his friendship and counsel. Till we meet again, *Hamba kahle, Xhamela. Qhawe la ma Qhawe!'* (Go well, rest in peace, Xhamela. Hero among heroes.)

At the funeral, he smiled as he stood and waved while thousands called his name. His intentions were clear: we are here not to mourn but to celebrate the life of a great man. 'In the last few years we have walked this road with greater frequency,' he said. 'To bid farewell to the veterans of our movement, paying our last respects to the fallen spears of the nation a generation now reaching the end of a long and heroic struggle. Those of us who are singled out to stay the longest bear the pain of seeing our comrades go.'

Some time later, when his grief was not so raw, he confessed to a radio station that when he had first arrived in Johannesburg he had been warned, 'Don't get involved with that man Walter Sisulu. If you do, you will spend the rest of your life in jail.' 'Of course,' said Mandela, 'I ignored this advice.'

By the time Albertina died at the age of 92 in 2011, Mandela, who was nearing 93, was no longer able to attend the funeral, never mind make the eulogy. His legs and feet, which for many years had given him pain while walking, now refused to make the journey. Instead, his wife,

ABOVE: Mandela had a soft spot for pop legend Michael Jackson, who was a generous donor to the Nelson Mandela Children's Fund.

RIGHT: South African-born, Oscar-winning actress Charlize Theron meets with Mandela at the Nelson Mandela Foundation in Johannesburg, in 2004.

164

Graça Machel, read a statement for him; for Mandela, who was best man at the Sisulu wedding, this death was particularly hard to bear. He referred to her as 'one of the greatest South Africans'. Albertina kept her family together while Walter was in prison for 26 years, and the power of her as a mother was seen in the distress of her children, all of whom had achieved significant positions.

In a far sadder tribute than the one he had paid to Walter Sisulu, Mandela, acknowledging that his own time was growing short, said: 'The years have taken the toll as one by one friends and comrades passed on. Every time it seems as part of oneself is being cut off, none of those cuts could have been more painful than the loss of this dear friend, you, my beloved sister.'

The death of Albertina gave Mandela much to reflect upon; while Walter Sisulu came out of prison and drifted almost seamlessly into the bosom of his large and loving family, Mandela had a somewhat lonelier path. He wanted nothing more than a relationship like that enjoyed by the Sisulus. Walter and Albertina adored each other. In one television interview, they appeared to forget the interviewer was there. Albertina paused for a while and looked at Walter. 'You want to kiss me, don't you?' she said to him. He, beaming with love, replied to his 80-year-plus love, 'Yes I do,' and kissed her lingeringly on the lips.

While Mandela's marriage to Graça Machel is happy, the many demands on him eroded the family time he treasures. As an iconic figure his life after prison was never his own, and although he tried to carve private space it was always difficult; there was always another who claimed they were a 'special case'. He became saddened too that the high hopes of democracy were obscured.

South Africa's progress, so inspiring in the immediate years after democracy, became erratic; inequity greater than under apartheid.

Before democratic elections, churchmen and women often invoked the biblical maxim of Isaiah for 'swords to be turned into ploughshares', but as days and months progressed into years in the 21st century, and as more political figures were revealed as tainted by corruption, another verse from Isaiah was invoked:

Your princes are rebels
And companions of thieves.
Every one loves a bribe
And runs after gifts.
They do not defend the fatherless,
And the widow's cause does not
Come to them.

One of the most difficult things is not to change society – but to change yourself.

Nelson Mandela

In July 2011, Zwelinzima Vavi, the head of the powerful two-million-member Congress of South African Trade Unions, condemned a 'powerful, corrupt, predatory elite combined with a conservative populist agenda [that had] harness[ed] the ANC to advance their interests.' Vavi referred to, 'wild zigzagging in the political direction of the country'.

He criticised growing poverty and joblessness. A million jobs had been lost in the three years preceding his speech – unemployment was officially around 26 percent, and at least double that unofficially. But BMWs and Mercedes were still conspicuous by their prevalence on the roads. And crime was rampant: 49 murders a day (an improvement on previous years), a rape every 26 seconds ...

None of this would have surprised the remarkable documenter of *Democracy in America*, Alexis de Tocqueville, who more than two centuries before observed that:

All revolutions enlarge the ambition of men ... In this first burst of triumph nothing seems impossible to anyone: not only are desires boundless, but the power of satisfying them seems almost boundless, too ... It must be recollected, moreover, that the people who destroy an aristocracy have lived under its laws; they have witnessed its splendour, and they have unconsciously imbibed the feelings and notions which it entertained. Thus at the moment when an aristocracy is dissolved, its spirit still pervades the mass of the community, and its tendencies are retained long after it has been defeated ... A sense of instability remains ... desires still remain extremely enlarged, when the means of satisfying them are diminished day by day.

Perhaps the betrayal felt by the so many who fought for liberation is misplaced, as the harm of decades cannot be overturned in two decades, yet still ... still the failures burn holes in hearts, they sadden, and as they intensified, an aging Nelson Mandela withdrew into himself and finally became silent.

Perhaps one could muse that Mandela's epitaph might one day be: I am, because of others. I learned all that I know from the greatest minds and the humblest of souls; all schooled me. I loved passionately, and was wounded deeply, and that taught me patience, tolerance, empathy and gratitude.

My dignity was denigrated, and through that I learned to walk tall, with pride, because personal dignity is contained within the spirit. I bent to hear the whispers of children, and heard wisdom. I listened to my enemies with my heart and not my ego, and, from that, learned how to manage their fears and build within them the confidence that overturned hatred and brought my people, and the people of other lands, to freedom.

I learned that freedom is not liberation; it is not the frivolous squandering of hours. True freedom is eternal duty in the protection and building of liberty.

And so we say to Mandela:

Sala kahle, Madiba. Siyabonga, Tata. (Stay well, Madiba. Thank you, father.)

Index

Photographic credits

AZ=Anna Zieminski BP=The Bigger Picture FvH=Friedrich von Hörsten GH=George Hallett GI=Gallo Images GM=Greg Marinovich IOA=Images of Africa JdP=Jéan du Plessis JS=Jürgen Schadeberg/www.jurgenschadeberg.com LG=Louise Gubb MA=UWC Robben Island Museum Mayibuye Archives PN=PictureNet RB= Rodger Bosch

Front cover: Theana Calitz/Foto24/GI; Pages: 1–6 BP; 7 GI; 15 JS; 16–19 MA; 21 Cape Archives; 23 MA; 24 JS; 25 MA; 26 all GI; 27–32 MA; 33 GI; 35–7 MA; 38 BP; 40 MA; 41 GI; 42 MA; 44–7; 48 BP; 49 Unknown photographer; 50 PN/HF; 51 PN/courtesy Nicodemus Sono; 52 JdP; 53 MA; 54 LG; 55 GI/*Rapport*/Helen McDonald; 56-9 BP; 61 GI; 62–5 MA; 67 FvH/IOA; 68 MA; 70 AZ; 72 GI; 75 JS; MA; 77 JS; 78 BP; 81–2 MA; 85 GI; 86 AZ; 88 GI; 89 MA; 90–1 GI; 92 LG; 95 MA; 96 GI; 99 BP; 100 MA; 103 PN/Ken Oosterbroek; 104 RB; 106 PN/Adil Bradlow; 109 Unknown photographer; 110 LG; 112 GM; 113 Eric Miller; 114 GI; 115 PN/João Silva; 116 GI; 119 GI; 120 LG; 121 both RB; 122 BP; 125 GI; 126–9 LG; 130 GI; 132 PN/Denis Farrell; 133 LG; 134–5 LG; 136 GH; 138 GI; 141GH; 142 GI; 143 GH; 145 JdP; 146 GI; 147 *The Argus*; 148 GI; 151 BP; 152 all GI; 153 PN/Shaun Harris; 155 GI; 156–7 BP; 158 GM; 159 GI; 160–1 BP/Reuters; 162 BP; 163 LG; 164 left BP, right GI/Getty Images, BP; 165 John Robinson; 166 PN/ Tim Zielenbach; 167 all GI

Bibliography

This book was put together as a result of interviews, discussions and readings over a number of years with numerous South African figures, amongst them President Nelson Mandela. My life has been enriched by knowing, and in some instances having been the friend of, many great South Africans. Some of their recollections filter through into my work, but overall the work is mine. I have been blessed with important friendships, including those with Helen Joseph, Tokyo Sexwale and Dali Tambo. Their reflections over the years have brought wisdom and, I hope, sensitivity, into my life and work. There were also interviews and discussions with key African National Congress leaders, Inkatha Freedom Party officials and others, people who did not wish attribution, but their contributions nonetheless helped guide my thinking and writing. This tribute to one of the greatest men of the twentieth century does not profess to be complete; time will bestow its own honours and great researchers. However, it contains more original research than any book published previously on this great man.

RESEARCH ESTABLISHMENTS:
Where no reference is made to a research establishment, the book, document or interview forms part of my own personal collection.
- Mayibuye Centre, University of the Western Cape, Cape Town (MC)
- South African Library, Cape Town (SAL)
- Personal collection, Barry Feinberg (BF)

BOOKS:
African Way, The, Mike Boon, Zebra, 1996
Beyond the Barricades, Popular resistance in South Africa, Kliptown books, 1991 (BF)
Bram Fischer, Afrikaner Revolutionary, Stephen Clingman, David Philip, 1997
Chained Together, Mandela, De Klerk and the Struggle to Remake South Africa, David Ottaway, Random House, 1993
Habla Nelson Mandela, Pathfinder Press, NY USA, 1986 (SAL)
In the Words of Nelson Mandela, edited by Jennifer Crwys-Williams, Penguin, 1998
Legacy of Apartheid, The, edited by Joseph Harker, Guardian newspapers, 1994
Long Walk to Freedom (autobiography) Nelson Mandela, MacDonald Purnell, 1994
Mandela, Ronald Harwood, Channel 4, 1987 (SAL)
Mandela, Echoes of an Era, Alf Kumalo, text by Es'kia Mphahlele, Penguin, 1990, (SAL)
Mandela's Five years of Freedom: South African Politics, Economics and Social Issues, 1990–1995, compiled by Elna Schoeman, Jacqueline A Kalley and Naomi Musiker, SAIIA, Biographical series no. 29, Vol. 10, 1996 (SAL)
Nelson Mandela, Mary Benson, Penguin Books, 1986
Nelson Mandela and Apartheid, Petero Nangoli, New Horizon, 1978, (SAL)
Nelson Mandela and the rise of the ANC, Jürgen Schadeberg, Jonathan Ball and AD Donker Publishers, 1990 (SAL)
Nelson Mandela Speaks, David Philip, Mayibuye Books and Pathfinder, 1993 (BF)
Nelson Mandela Speeches 1990, Intensify the Struggle to Abolish Apartheid, edited by Greg McCartan, Pathfinder Press, 1990
Nelson Mandela, symbol of resistance and hope for a free South Africa, edited by ES Reddy, Namedia Foundation, Sterling Publishers, New Delhi, India, 1990 (SAL)

Nelson Rolihlahla Mandela, Two Historic Speeches, Learn and Teach Publications, 1990
Opposition in South Africa, the leadership of ZK Matthews, Nelson Mandela and Stephen Biko, Tim M Juckes, Praeger, 1996
Patterns of Violence, Case Studies of Conflict in Natal, edited by Anthony Minnaar, HSRC Publishers, 1992
Robben Island, Charlene Smith, Struik and Mayibuye Books, 1997 (and associated interviews and research)
Robben Island, the Reunion, Mayibuye Books, 1996
Satyagraha in South Africa, Mohandas Gandhi, Navajivan Publishing House, Ahmedabad, 1928
Struggle for Liberation in South Africa, The, Govan Mbeki, Mayibuye and David Philip, 1992
Sunset at Midday, Govan Mbeki, Nolwazi, 1996
Walden on Heroes, BBC, 1998

NEWSPAPERS AND MAGAZINES
'Stop Aids nonsense – Mandela tells Mbeki's government to halt debates and fight the war' by Ranjeni Munusamy, Sunday Times, 17 February 2002
'Mbeki's grand plan makes the grade' by Justice Malala, Sunday Times, 30 June 2002
'The one-time mass movement now serves the elite' by Sean Jacobs and Jonathan Faull, Sunday Times, 27 April 2003
'Thabo Mbeki: The Chief; I play the man I am' by Mark Gevisser, Sunday Times, 20 June 1999
'Person of the Century – The Sacred Warrior' by Nelson Mandela, Time, January 3, 2000
'Aids war needs leaders' by Edwin Lombard, Sunday Times, 2 December 2001
'Mandela' by Richard Stengel, Time, 9 May 1994
'The Cape of poverty', Mail & Guardian, 13 May 2003
'A Third World dreamer, or a man who will change history?' by Mondli Makhanya and Carol Paton, Sunday Times, April 2002

RESOURCE MATERIALS:
Agreements entered into between the African National Congress and the South African government at the summit meeting held on 26 September 1992 (SAL)
ANC London, Box 50 (MC)
ANC, Lusaka conference reports 1985. (MC)
ANC Lusaka Secretary-General NEC (ILC) meetings 1990 to 1991 (52.1 to 52.6) (MC)
ANC Lusaka, Secretary General NEC (NWC) Minutes, 1986 to 1990 (51.1 to 51.5) (MC)
ANC National preparatory committee documents of the National Consultative Conference, Lusaka, 1985 (MC)
ANC NEC January 8 statement, 1996, delivered by Nelson Mandela
ANC NEC statement, January 8, 1991, delivered by deputy president, Nelson Mandela (SAL)
Dawn, journal of Umkhonto we Sizwe, MK 25th anniversary (MC)
Empty Talk while the Country Burns, United democratic Front pamphlet, 1991 (SAL)
Freedom, Justice and Dignity for all in South Africa, statements and articles by Mr Nelson Mandela, president of the African National Congress of South Africa, issued by the Centre against Apartheid, Department of Political and Security Council Affairs, 1978 (SAL)
Groote Schuur Minute, The, May 1990 (SAL)
Invest in Peace, addresses by the President of the Republic of South Africa, Mr Nelson Mandela to the United Nations General Assembly and to the joint houses of the congress of the United States of America, October 1994

Is there a National Agenda – and who sets it? Thabo Mbeki, Prestige Lecture, University of Port Elizabeth, 1995 (SAL)
Land Hunger, Liberation, February, 1956 (SAL)
Letter from Nelson Mandela to Mrs Manorama Bhalla, secretary of the Indian Council for cultural relations, New Delhi, 3 August 1980 (SAL)
Letter from Dr Uwe Kaestner, the ambassador to South Africa of the Federal Republic of Germany, 27 May 1998
Mandela: U.S. wants holocaust – CNN.com, 30 January, 2003
Message of condolence from Nelson and Winnie Mandela to the Mozambican people, the Machel family, Frelimo and the Mozambican government on the occasion of the death of Samora Machel, October 1986 (SAL)
Nelson Mandela addresses the Special Committee Against Apartheid, United Nations, 22 June 1990 (SAL)
Nelson Mandela, letter 3 August 1980, on Acceptance of the Jawaharlal Nehru Award for International Understanding for 1979, United Nations Centre Against Apartheid (SAL)
Nelson Mandela, The People's Leader, issued by UNB, MSRC, an Asoso affiliate, 1983 (SAL)
No Easy Walk to Freedom, presidential address by Nelson R Mandela, ANC (Transvaal), 21 September 1953 (SAL)
People are destroyed, Liberation, October, 1955 (SAL)
Pretoria Minute, The, 6 August 1990 (SAL)
South Africa's Freedom Struggle, Yusuf Dadoo, Kliptown books, 1990
Shifting Sands of Illusion, The, Liberation, June 1953 (SAL)
Slovo The Unfinished Autobiography, Ravan Press, 1995
Tribute to Nelson Mandela, by Mac Maharaj, 4 June 1998
University of Zimbabwe, Addresses and Orations on the occasion of the conferment of the degree of Doctor of Law on Nelson Rolihlahla Mandela, 6/7 June 1986 (SAL)

INTERVIEWS, DISCUSSIONS:
My own files, notebooks and tape recordings of interviews, discussions, meetings, conferences and the ilk over more than two decades of journalism.
- Interviews Amin Cajee, since 1986
- Interviews Helen Joseph, since 1982
- Email communications Zelda la Grange, April 2003
- Various Nelson Mandela, since 13 February 1990, and also press conferences
- Indres Naidoo, 2, 8, 9 June 1998
- Parliament, 3 June 1998
- Alan Fine, 8 June 1998
- Su Vos, 8, 15 June 1998
- Jay Naidoo, 8 June 1998
- Zamindlela Zama, 15 June 1998
- Patrick Lekota, 9 June 1998
- Barry Streek, 10 June 1998
- Mangosuthu Buthelezi, 9 June 1998
- Truth and Reconciliation Commission hearings into chemical and biological warfare, Cape Town, 10, 11, 12 June 1998
- Govan Mbeki, 12 June 1998
- Archbishop Desmond Tutu, 18 June 1988